THE ENVIRONMENTAL DESTRUCTION
OF SOUTH FLORIDA

The Environmental Destruction of South Florida

A Handbook for Citizens

Edited by
William Ross McCluney

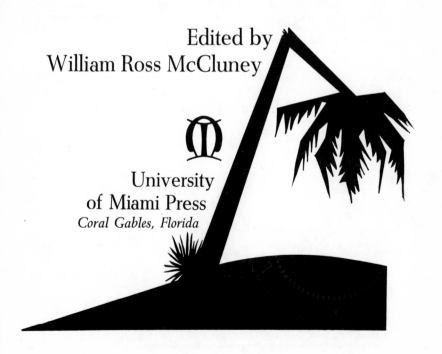

University
of Miami Press
Coral Gables, Florida

CONTENTS

Dedicated to the memory of
Hans Frohlich

PREFACE

As the 1970-1971 winter season began in South Florida, water levels in the Everglades and in the water conservation areas were already several feet below normal. Numerous Glades fires had already begun and the Flood Control District warned us that we might have to face water rationing in the coming months. Even though the Saga development fight had ended in South Dade County, numerous other large developments loomed all over South Florida. The Dade County Chamber of Commerce was pushing to retain the old jetport site and started reviving an old seaport proposal for South Dade. The Dade County Manager had a team studying the county's waste disposal problems. The sugarcane fields south of Lake Okeechobee were burning and filling the air with dense smoke. Large-scale subsidy of bus transportation was being planned for Miami. The war on pollution of South Florida waters was continuing with most of Dade's canals already so polluted as to be unsafe for swimming.

These are just some of the many environmental crises facing South Florida. At stake is the health and survival of the region and its inhabitants. There is little doubt that unless some rather drastic changes are made in the way we are doing things, South Florida will be transformed into an environmental wasteland, with a loss of the things which make the area a beautiful and enjoyable place to live.

The purpose of this book is twofold. First, to alert the public to the growing danger of massive environmental destruction which is threatening the area. Second, to provide basic factual information about the environment of South Florida and the way it is being destroyed. Although the book is intended as an environmental handbook, tailored to the problems of South Florida, its reading should be but a first step in one's attempt to acquire a greater understanding of the problems. It is hoped that the book will provide sufficient background information on current issues so that the reader will be able to understand most of the environmentally oriented articles that he may read in the newspapers or in magazines. The goal is to produce better-informed, more effective citizens.

There is hardly a national or global environmental issue which does not affect South Florida, as, for example oil spills, pesticides, and the SST. Many of these are well-covered in newspapers, magazines, and books, and no attempt was made to include them here. Wherever possible, the problems peculiar to South Florida are emphasized. All the authors contributing to the book (with the exception of Gene Marine) are or have been residents of this area and share our common concern that its beauty and other amenities be preserved.

Since most of the authors live in Dade County, there is an admitted emphasis on its problems, at a risk of possible exclusion of equally important problems in other adjacent South Florida counties. However, all of these counties share similar environmental problems, so that most references to Dade County are applicable to the other counties as well.

Everyone who lives in South Florida and therefore decides its future should be familiar with the facts behind our environmental degradation. Every schoolchild should be familiar with the history of man's alteration of the landscape and the other resources of the area. Few are. Often residents of Denver and San Francisco can tell us more of the facts about the disruption of our natural ecosystem than can the local residents.

No wonder there is a frequent slowness to action on the part of local citizens when the region is threatened by some new ecological crisis. We have the additional disadvantage of a constant influx of new residents—refugees from harsher climates—who are not yet familiar with Florida problems and who are therefore insensitive to the indicators of future disaster. Ignorant of a century of exploitation and the present precariousness of the natural balance, these newcomers leap in to advocate development of Florida as though it were a New Frontier, impervious to damage. We are only gradually coming to an awareness of our common interest as a community of survivors, living on a small finger of land jutting out several hundred miles into the sea. Let us join in a concerted effort to mend our destructive ways and to seek the preservation of a healthy environment for ourselves and for every other living thing.

Coral Gables, February 1971   Ross McCluney

ACKNOWLEDGMENTS

I wish to acknowledge the help that was given to me in the development of this book. I was supported during the major part of the work by a graduate assistantship from the Center for Urban and Environmental Studies of the University of Miami, and I particularly wish to thank Dr. Joseph G. Hirschberg and Dr. Carl E. B. McKenry for making this possible.

I also wish to thank the Research Council of the University of Miami for advancing the funds to help finance the initial printing of 2,000 copies of the book.

Without the contributions from the various authors this book, of course, would not have been possible. Robert Carrodus and Glenn Frye are also gratefully acknowledged for their help in drawing the maps in Dr. Craighead's article.

Finally, I wish to thank Arthur Marshall and Polly Redford for their many helpful suggestions for improving the manuscript.

Coral Gables, Florida   Ross McCluney
February 1971

We are using the earth as if we were the last generation.

JULIA ALLEN FIELD

THE SPACESHIP EARTH

C. Richard Tillis

WE LIVE IN A WORLD that is doubling its human population every thirty-seven years.

WE LIVE IN A WORLD that is doubling the size of its industrial complex every ten years. This means that by the year 2007 we will have twice as many people and thirteen times as much industry with perhaps thirteen times as much air and water pollution.

WE LIVE IN A WORLD in which jet aircraft approaching and leaving our airports burn 1,000 pounds of fossil fuel in ten minutes, converting them into 2,000 pounds of water and 1,500 pounds of carbon dioxide gas, while at the same time we are rushing to pave over the land, destroying the vegetation which could utilize this added carbon dioxide, restoring the air we breathe to its normal condition.

WE LIVE IN A WORLD in which right now DDT and other persistent pesticides are falling out of our atmosphere into our oceans and reducing the ability of microscopic plants called phytoplankton to photosynthesize, grow, and produce oxygen. This may not seem too important until we realize that these microscopic plants produce ninety-one percent of the oxygen which we must have to breathe to live!

WE LIVE IN A WORLD—a nation—in which the people in approximately three-fourths of our states carry twelve parts per million DDT in their bodies. The Federal Food and Drug Administration will not allow milk to be sold which contains more than five parts DDT per million. A mother nursing her child in Florida could very well be administering more than twice the DDT to her child than FDA regulations will permit.

WE LIVE IN A WORLD in which our larger industrial cities are

Mr. Tillis was formerly director of the Pine Jog Conservation Education Center in West Palm Beach. He recently became the state's first consultant in environmental education.

receiving rain more often on weekdays than weekends. This seems fine for the picnickers until we realize that weekend reductions in soot and other particles from industrial stacks (because of less production on weekends) are the apparent reason for less rain on weekends. The frightening thing is that scientists, capable enough to put men on the moon, have not been able to change our weather to any appreciable degree intentionally, but here we are changing it unintentionally.

WE LIVE IN A WORLD whose average annual temperature has been changed by 1.9 degrees since 1890. Based on this increase we can expect a 9 degree change by 2020. A 9 degree increase would perhaps begin melting the polar icecaps—raising our shorelines—inundating parts of Florida.

WE LIVE IN A STATE whose weather and climate has changed considerably in the past sixty years. We have reason to suspect that man's modification of Florida's normal water drainage systems has created this change. We were warned as much as thirty years ago that destruction of the Everglades would lead to an increase in frost days in South Florida.

WE LIVE IN A WORLD in which many of the finest scientists in the world: Barry Commoner of Washington University of St. Louis, Lamont Cole of Cornell, Henry Nehrling of Connecticut College for Women, and many others, are predicting that if we continue to live our lives just as we are today with no sudden changes, *human life will no longer exist on this earth 100 years from today!*

If man is to have a future on earth we must begin to utilize established scientific principles to provide a better environment now and in the future. The tools are readily available. What we must have is the people demanding their use.

The earth has been brought to its knees because of a conflict between two systems of economics: One, the economics of man, is familiar to everyone, truck driver to bank president. The other, the economics of nature, a comprehension of the hows and whys of the great flows of matter and energy on our earth which produce life and death, storm and serenity, drought and flood, is completely foreign to the American public. We have failed miserably in any efforts to teach this economics of nature to our youth, just as our parents failed to teach it to us. The economics of man is supported by, and is totally dependent on, the economics of nature. Yet, every conservation issue is simply a conflict between these two great systems of economics. With a public colossally ignorant of nature's economics, it is not surprising that the economics of man has won out in almost every conflict with those of nature. This has brought us to our present state.

Our only hope for the future is that we can educate the public sufficiently in the economics of nature to produce decisions on the use of our land, water, air, minerals, plants, and animals, decisions which recognize the importance of the economics of nature and utilize them to provide a sustained yield of these precious entities. Perhaps this booklet can begin this important job.

In April 1970, the world held its breath as three American astronauts faced the greatest threat man can imagine. Their life support system was not functioning! The electrically-driven, electronically-controlled machinery which removed excess carbon dioxide and poisonous gases from their air, poisons from their water supply, and controlled the moisture content and temperature of their vehicle was not working. Fortunately, by using the lunar landing vehicle's power and life support system, these three men made it back to earth.

This dramatic event reminded us that for these men to live, they had to return to earth. The materials and conditions on earth which they had to have to live are our natural resources. The conservation lesson was dramatic. We should pursue this line of thought further and realize that our earth has its own life support system, infinitely more effective and dependable than any system NASA has devised. This system of which I speak is a *living* life support system, made up of plants and animals from microscopic to gigantic in dimension. Considering it will introduce us to nature's economics.

When a part breaks down in the life support system of a spaceship, men's lives are in immediate danger. The capsule cannot grow another part. On earth we have destroyed many parts of our life support system; the passenger pigeon is a well-known example. Yet, because of the design and complexity of our living life support system, it continues to perform and man can still breathe, drink, eat, and live within the temperature and humidity ranges on our earth.

We must learn to appreciate the economics of nature and its resultant living life support system. Great scientists are citing evidence that unless we stop polluting our air and water and destroying the "living parts" of our life-support system, we are in danger of extinction.

I hope you have traveled with me into the tunnel of gloom. I also hope you have seen the light at the end of the tunnel. That light is a

3

promise that if man learns to appreciate and act within the economics of nature, to conserve and maintain his living life-support system, he can look forward to a glorious future assisted by science and technology, augmented by knowledge, and guided by a new sensitivity to the life needs of all earth's creatures, including his fellow man.

IS MAN DESTROYING SOUTH FLORIDA?

F. C. Craighead, Sr.

I have been asked to write around the theme "Are We Destroying South Florida? " It seems more appropriate to title the remarks that follow: "Have We Destroyed South Florida? " Certainly when we consider the changes that have taken place in these natural environments since the turn of the century the latter title is more appropriate.

The destruction and near elimination of many natural plant communities from Lake Okeechobee to Cape Sable form an awesome picture of misdirected progress. This destruction proceeded so rapidly that in most cases only the descriptions of the early naturalists are now available to reconstruct the picture of what existed when white man came to settle here. No one living today can expect to see the restoration of those magnificent plant communities that inspired the early botanists and naturalists visiting the area around 1900.

Hugh M. Smith, in his 1896 report for the U.S. Fish Commission on the resources of Biscayne Bay, described its crystal clear waters, including those of several creeks that enter the bay from the Everglades. He mentioned that tons of fish were being taken, that crocodiles (some as long as sixteen feet) were common, and that 50,000 alligator hides were shipped in 1894.

It was not until about 1920 that the changes were recognized and recorded by several early naturalists, including John Kunkel Small, Charles Torrey Simpson, and Thomas Barbour. Small, who had been in the area since 1900, wrote in his book *From Eden to Sahara, Florida's Tragedy* (1929): "The wholesale devastation of the plant covering, through carelessness, thoughtlessness, and vandalism in the Peninsular State, prehistoric and historic, was everywhere apparent. This reckless,

Dr. Craighead, a forest entomologist with the U.S. Department of Agriculture for 38 years, has been actively involved in a number of ecological studies and is presently a consulting ecologist with the Center for Urban and Environmental Studies of the University of Miami.

even wanton, devastation has now gained such headway that the future of North America's most prolific paradise seems to spell DESERT."

Simpson, writing in 1932 in his second book about Florida, *Florida Wild Life,* closed with a prediction: "Looking back to the days when South Florida was a beautiful wilderness filled with magnificent wild life and then contemplating the wreck of today, is enough to sicken the heart of a lover of nature, yes, even of any sensible person who has a true valuation of the useful and beautiful. If things go on here as they have done in the past few years this can only end in the destruction of all that is lovely and of value that nature has bestowed on us."

Barbour, in his interesting book *A Vanishing Eden,* published in 1944, stated, "A large part of Florida is now so devastated that many of her friends are disinclined to believe that she ever could have been the paradise which I know once existed."

I was fortunate to get a glimpse of subtropical Florida in 1917 when I visited Paradise Key, then a state park established by the Association of Women's Clubs of Florida and now called Royal Palm Hammock. From there my travels took me to Lake Okeechobee, where I was entranced with the remaining custard apple swamps. A fisherman took me across Lake Okeechobee to Moore Haven. This was ten years before the great hurricane that broke the Lake Okeechobee dam and wiped out over 2,000 lives. The tremendous agricultural possibilities of these rich soils were just coming to be appreciated. From Moore Haven I walked to LaBelle, where I hobnobbed for some days with a beekeeper and then took the paddlewheel steamer down the Caloosahatchee River to Fort Myers. At that time I did not realize the full import of the destruction under way. I was lost in the vastness of what I saw and, like many others, thought what I saw would last forever. I still retain vivid impressions of that trip—the tropical verdure of Paradise Key, the cool watery tunnels under the leafy canopies of the custard apple swamps, the overhanging trees along the bends of the sinuous Caloosahatchee River, their branches festooned with myriads of orchids and bromeliads. By the time I was able to move to South Florida thirty years later, much that was not good was sadly obvious.

Southern Florida, A Great Ecosystem

Southern Florida from Lake Okeechobee to Florida Bay and the Gulf of Mexico was once one of nature's great masterpieces. Here a massive swamp had been created between east and west coastal ridges,

*South Florida, showing the historical location of the Everglades
and the Big Cypress Swamp.*

7

plugged by a forest of mangroves at its southern tip and filled with water several feet deep during the rainy season. This swamp supported a lush vegetation that in turn deposited a rich organic soil, which provided nutrients for a fantastic population of animals. The copious rainfall soaked the peaty soil and moved slowly through the vegetation, and the excess finally came to rest in the largest known freshwater reservoir, the Biscayne aquifer, a porous limestone underground layer, some ten to forty feet thick. While hurricanes and freezes here and there destroyed patches of the supporting vegetation, and droughts and subsequent lightning fires left scars, these had little effect on the whole, which was maintained in relative equilibrium over five thousand years by a variety of forces, some building, some destroying. It took man, with his plans to better nature's design, to destroy in fifty years what she had maintained for several thousand years.

Notwithstanding all these modifications and "improvements" to save lives and enhance agriculture, in March-April of 1970 the lowered farmlands for twenty-five miles south of Lake Okeechobee were flooded by heavy rains that destroyed much of the planted crops. And so it will be again and again in this man-dominated ecosystem, until we realize that so little has been gained by these efforts that we should resign ourselves to accept nature's plan and attempt restoration of the marvelously balanced ecosystem of seventy years ago.

Within this ecosystem are three conspicuous subdivisions, containing distinct types of vegetation herein described: an extensive saw grass marsh covering the eastern half, a somewhat smaller cypress swamp forming the western portion, and the saline mangrove crescent to the south.

The Everglades—The River of Grass

The eastern portion of the South Florida ecosystem began around Lake Okeechobee and extended to the Gulf in a gently sloping drainage path over 100 miles long and at places forty miles wide. It included the farmland around the lake extending south to Levee 5, all of Conservation Areas 1, 2, and 3, and the Shark River Slough, now within the Everglades National Park. Formerly the Everglades collected rainfall from over 3,000 square miles of marshland, and at times of heavy downpour some overflow from Lake Okeechobee fed this drainage runoff. The water moved so slowly—retarded by its grassy bed and a slope of only two inches per mile—that the movement of the water

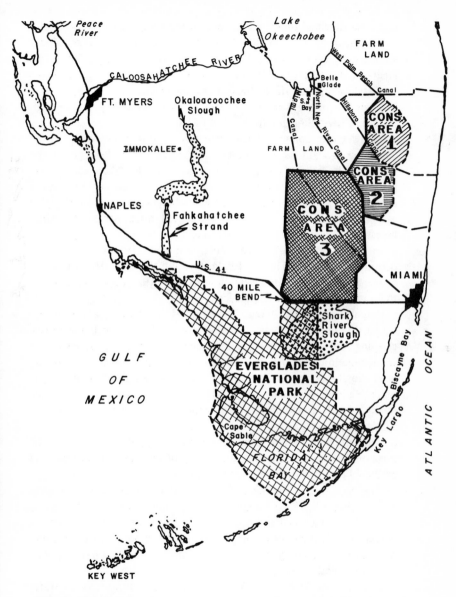

South Florida, showing water conservation areas of the Central and Southern Florida Flood Control District and the boundaries of the Everglades National Park.

9

could be detected only by the trend of the submerged, vinelike water weeds. Much of it evaporated. More was used by plants. The remainder seeped into the thick peat beds and the Biscayne aquifer. When this great marshy lake was full to overflowing, the excess water cut across the eastern coastal ridge through several creeks into Biscayne Bay, through the spillways across the pineland into Florida Bay, and through the Shark River Slough into the Gulf of Mexico.

Man's greed dominated his evaluation of this great marsh. All he could see beneath its clear waters were acres of rich, level peat to be farmed. All early planning centered on draining. The many creeks carrying off excess water were blasted out, canals were cut through the coastal ridge, and the meandering Caloosahatchee with its overhanging gardens was straightened into a wide, deep ditch banked by white limestone glaring in the winter sunshine.

Suddenly many unforeseen events took place. The excess water ran off quickly to the Atlantic, Florida Bay, and the Gulf. The winter dry season was prolonged by several months, and little or no water stood in the survival holes of the Everglades.

Aquatic animals suffered. The clear, slowly-moving water was no longer filtered through saw grass. It now rushed through the canals, carrying tons of muck that filled the coastal bays and lakes, destroying the fishing industry. The peat beds dried far below the usual depth and were slowly consumed by fires that smoldered for months in the punk-like soil. Gradually the great "sponge" turned to ashes on the pinnacle rock foundation, which protruded at many places in the southern part of the area.

The farmlands around Lake Okeechobee began to sink. By 1937 the agronomists pointed out that a lowering of six feet had occurred and predicted that it would continue to bedrock.

The basic link in the life chain failed. The final straw was the levee built during 1962-1965 completely across the Shark River Slough. A severe drought ensued and no gates were opened to provide water for Everglades National Park until Conservation Area 3 filled in 1966. Naturalists the country over became alarmed. Scarcely a newspaper or magazine failed to feature the death of the Everglades.

The great battle, termed "Water for Birds and Alligators versus Water for People?" was on. It lasted until the copious rainfalls of late 1966 and 1967 filled the slough and has been ominously silent since then, even though the excess water, unable to drain naturally, has caused widespread destruction of vegetation and animal life.

10

The Big Cypress Swamp

The Big Cypress Swamp comprises most of Collier and a considerable part of Monroe County. It is a self-sufficient ecological unit that
supplies nutrient waters to the Gulf mangrove swamps. This big swamp
is distinct in many ways from the saw grass Everglades, the River of
Grass. It exists because its foundation is a relatively impervious bedrock
of sandy limestone etched by sloughs, basins, and potholes and often
outcropping to pine or hammock growth. The low places are filled with
a variety of shallow soils, marl, sand, muck, and peat, supporting
characteristic vegetation such as cypress, bay heads, wet prairies, and
custard apple and pop ash swamps. Heavy precipitation runs off in a
sheet of water six to twenty-four inches deep. The remainder slowly
seeps seaward or becomes pooled in the depressions holding the porous
sands and spongy peats where it is slowly utilized in the dry season.

On the deep sands in the vicinity of Immokalee, the highest lands of
the Big Cypress, a substantial agriculture has developed. These sands are
capable of surface drainage by canals and pumps. On the shallow soils
elsewhere in the Big Cypress most efforts at farming have failed from
drought or excessive flooding.

The Fahkahatchee Strand or Slough, some four by twenty miles in
area, is one of the prized features of the Big Cypress. This swamp once
fostered two beautiful plant communities, one of great cypress trees
standing in water, another of even taller (some 125 feet) royal palms
overtopping a variety of tropical hardwoods growing on slightly higher
islands.

West of the Fahkahatchee Strand these sands deepen and merge into
the coastal dunes where several cities, Fort Myers, Naples, and Marco,
have developed. They form a valuable aquifer which if properly
managed may support a much larger population. However, in the past
five years this sandy region has been dissected by miles of canals
opening into the Gulf of Mexico.

Logging of the giant cypress trees (often six feet in diameter and 100
feet tall) was begun in the forties, and by 1950 all of the commercially
valuable cypress had been removed. Fires raged through the logging
debris and crept through the peat in dry years, destroying the remaining
trees. Likewise, many of the tropical tree islands were destroyed but
miraculously many of the royal palms escaped. During the drought
periods of 1962 and 1965, much of the wild land of Collier and western
Monroe counties burned. The Tamiami Trail became a stretch of

11

smoking embers from Forty Mile Bend to near Naples. Even some of the pinelands that had escaped 100 years of droughts and fires were left a charred mass of poles.

The difficulties of drainage in the Big Cypress have retarded man's mastery of the area, and there may be time to save this extensive swamp from the fate of the everglade marshes. This land is an asset for its wildlife, its hunting, fishing, and other recreation, and for limited agriculture. It should be properly classified and held in perpetuity with a minimum of development.

The Saline Mangrove Crescent

The remarkable mangrove forests that dominate the shoreline from Cape Canaveral around the tip of Florida to Cedar Keys on the west coast form one of the great natural resources in Florida. They are responsible for the deep peat beds that form a protective covering along the coasts. They protect the shoreline from erosion by storm tides and reduce the effects of violent hurricanes. Recent biological studies have shown that these estuarine areas are the source of much food and are the nursery grounds for our abundant marine life, sport and commercial fishes, and shellfish. The coastal rivers are the home of the vanishing manatee, or sea cow. Behind the landward margin of these swamps a low embankment has been built by the rising sea. This is called the Buttonwood Embankment. It impounds the extensive freshwater marshes and also permits a gradual overflow of this fresh water, thereby reducing the salinity. This lowered salinity is necessary to the normal growth of the plant and animal life of the estuaries.

The surface of the mangrove peat beds lies at about mean tide. It is alternately wet and dry with the diurnal tides. The more inland portions are flooded with fresh water during the summer rains and exposed during the dry winters. Thus organic matter is alternately accumulated while submerged and broken down when exposed into detritus and simple chemical products utilized for food by plants and animals. The productivity of these swamps has been shown to be greater than our best farmlands, and as such conservatively valued at over $300 per acre per year.

Fortunately, more than half of these estuarine swamps are in the Everglades National Park and will be preserved, provided that annual wetting by fresh waters is not curtailed. It is still not fully appreciated that these mangrove swamps and the associated animal life do require fresh water for their normal metabolism. Unfortunately, much of the swampland on the east and west coasts has already been destroyed by draglines and by bulkheading. Developers are now beginning to recognize the value of these estuaries to the well-being of the area. Hopefully, much of the remaining estuarine area may be saved and its productivity retained for the good of all.

Tropical Hardwood Hammocks

Within the South Florida ecosystem and its three general vegetative areas just described are numbers of delicately balanced plant communities or associations. One of the most attractive, and in many respects, one of the most interesting, is the tropical hardwood hammock. These hammocks, also called domes or houses, are scattered through the higher land on slight elevations of harder limestone pitted with solution holes. They are nearly circular in outline or are slightly elongated and dome-shaped. They maintain a uniform climate, cooler in summer, warmer and frost-proof in winter. A layer of hammock peat, an essential growth-promoting substance, covers their rocky floors. This humus mat supports over 150 species of trees, and a number of shrubs and lianas grow in the understory. Here also, or in the rock pits, are found some fifty ferns. But the greatest glory of these hammocks is the profusion of epiphytes covering the trees: sixteen species of bromeliads, or air plants, twenty-four orchids, and eighteen ferns.

What have we left today? Fires have run through and practically destroyed all of the hammocks in Everglades National Park. Several hammocks on Indian sites in the mangrove area, three mahogany hammocks, and the southern end of Paradise Key still retain some impression of a virgin forest, but lack several of their former species. Some few hammocks on the Dade County pineland between Miami and Homestead are fairly well preserved because they are located near old homes and were valued and protected by the occupants. The hammocks in western Monroe and Collier counties are somewhat better off, but the best of these, such as those in the Fahkahatchee Strand, are badly fire-scarred and have been vandalized to such an extent that several rare orchids and other plant species have disappeared.

The Alligator

The alligator dominated the freshwater marshes of South Florida much as did the buffalo on the Great Plains before white man appeared.

13

When abundant, the alligator occupied hundreds of thousands of water-retaining depressions in the shallowly covered bedrock. These holes, locally called gator holes or survival holes, were kept open from plant invasion by the activities of the reptiles. The resulting pools served as reservoirs for much of the aquatic life of the area. Thus the food chain of swamp life from one-celled plants and animals through tiny invertebrates and small food fishes to the dominating species of birds and animals was maintained. The loss of thousands of these survival holes through drainage and by the decimation of the alligator have had far-reaching effects on the disappearance of wading birds, otters, and numerous forms of smaller life.

The alligator also performed an important role in shaping the vegetation in and around the gator holes and especially in extending gator trails from the small creeks landward and in forming cross-connections through the saw grass between creeks.

Although much of the alligator habitat has been destroyed by drainage and is not likely to be restored, in the marginal swamp land bordering the Shark River Slough good recovery was noticed in 1969 and 1970. In the slough itself the high water maintained since 1966 destroyed nests and has driven the surviving alligators out because of inaccessible food in this vast lake. Even though fishes were abundant they were not available to the alligators. Those moving out to higher land were noted to be thin and emaciated.

The decline of the alligators came rapidly. Within Everglades National Park and vicinity, early droughts and fires around 1937 and 1952, plus poaching, began to have an accelerating effect. The writer made frequent trips on several freshwater creeks in the mid-fifties when it was not uncommon to count fifty to 100 alligators during the course of five to six hours of cruising. In 1965 and 1966 these same creeks were visited nearly every other week and not a single alligator was observed.

With knowledgeable management this reptile could respond rapidly and could again become a valuable interpretive subject in the Park. More importantly, it could become a valuable economic asset and a symbol to the surrounding community instead of a vanished species.

Shell Mounds and Florida Aborigines

Along both peninsular coasts and around the tip of Florida were hundreds of shell mounds, the homesites of several tribes of pre-

Columbian peoples that have completely vanished through the impact of the white man. The little we know of these resourceful people, who lived chiefly on products of the sea and estuaries, indicates a vigorous, strong race in harmony with a most rigorous environment. The great heaps of shells on which they lived were rapidly utilized for road building material as the white man advanced down the east and west coasts. Very few remain outside the Everglades National Park. Most of these within the Park were occupied by white men between 1830 and the establishment of the Park in 1947. The tropical forests on these mounds were cleared and the rich organic soils farmed until the end of the sailboat days. Much produce and charcoal were carried to Key West. Very few mounds have escaped this use. Let us hope that a thorough study of these remaining habitats will eventually be made and something more revealed of these vanished peoples.

Can Anything Be Done?

Yes, but it will take many years, much greater appreciation of the values involved, and inspired management by citizens and public officials.

Beginning at the coast, the remaining mangroves must be preserved along the shoreline as well as those bordering the inland creeks. These creeks should be left open to the sea. In several places in Dade, Collier, and Lee counties the importance of this mangrove fringe has been realized and plans have been adopted by a few developers to save much of it. Progress is being made. Mention should be made of the recently adopted plans for developing property bordering Biscayne Bay in Dade County, near Naples in Collier County, and in Lee County. On Sanibel Island, the Sanibel-Captiva Conservation Foundation has done a great deal in saving large blocks of mangroves, aided by the Conservation Foundation and the Nature Conservancy.

There is also a critical area along the inner edge of the saline swamps at the junction of the freshwater marshes. Much of the sheet flow of fresh water into these mangrove estuaries must be maintained.

Conservation Areas 1, 2, and 3 have been greatly modified from their original condition, but with proper water control they can be maintained as excellent fishing and recreation areas.

Water supplies for the Big Cypress from the Fahkahatchee east are dependent entirely on local rainfall. This water moves slowly into the estuarine areas in a sheet flow over a prolonged period. Canalization of

15

this area should be stopped immediately until a sound plan of management is prepared. This entire area will require a multiple use management plan, with the primary purpose the conserving of available water in its slow flow to the Gulf of Mexico.

Much of the area could be left in present ownership where cooperation on a common objective is possible. Possibly the greater part must come under state or federal control to accomplish good use management. Timber production, small farming, hunting, fishing, and other recreation would be the principal uses. Even small community developments would be possible.

Strict control to stop further development and battles to restrict rapid runoff of the numerous canals recently dredged in the deeper sands between the Fahkahatchee and the coastal dunes will be required. This water must be conserved to maintain this limited aquifer for the coastal towns.

Water requirements of the everglade marshes are provided by rainfall and a slow flow beginning south of the agricultural lands around Lake Okeechobee. Recently, supplemental water has poured into the conservation areas from Lake Okeechobee through the numerous canals and pumping stations. That flow going to the Everglades National Park must be regulated to the specifications of the Park biologists to provide a draw-down during the late winter and spring.

It must be realized that much of the Everglades National Park as well as the Big Cypress has always been dependent on rainfall rather than a flow from the north. Here plants and animals are adjusted to a winter-spring drought. Such communities should not be flooded during the dry period.

No more canals should be dug anywhere south of Lake Okeechobee until several years of observation can develop a revised watering plan to replace the hodgepodge that is destroying nature's ecosystems.

It is especially important to determine the cause of the lowered water table in the pinelands of the southeastern portion of the Everglades National Park and provide for the restoration of the feeding grounds for the once abundant wildlife of this area.

THE FUTURE OF FLORIDA'S SALT AND FRESHWATER RESOURCES

Arthur R. Marshall

In discussing the future of Florida's salt and freshwater resources, I have necessarily limited myself to an area which greatly affects those resources, which has been and is the subject of national environmental controversy, and is typical of the environmental problems we face—the Kissimmee-Okeechobee-Everglades Basin. The problems of this large area are those generated by our will to exercise man's dominion with very little regard to the inflexible and certain laws of the natural world.

It is time—well past time—that we abandoned the centuries-old belief that man's dominion over the earth includes its willful destruction. We can, of course, exercise that dominion and fry us all. A person whose views oppose mine would likely say that my comparison is unfair because in his philosophy, exercise of dominion excludes doing harm to others.

Before he settles in his views he should consider the harm—something less than holocaust—which exercise of dominion has brought to his fellows. He will, after searching diligently, struggle to define a critical difference.

Exercise of dominion has already brought great harm to millions of supposedly unaffected persons. At its worst in the *cities*, some examples are the eradicated green spaces, the traffic beast, people piled on people, polluted and virtually useless waters—air unfit for human consumption, and—last and least in my opinion—burdensome taxation to confront or repair the ills.

The harm also extends to the *countryside*—the diminishing wild things and places, polluted and virtually useless waters, loss of productive topsoils and even the mechanisms which produce them, people piled on people, the growing hollowness in the words of our

Mr. Marshall is an ecologist with the Center for Urban and Environmental Studies of the University of Miami. This chapter is the speech he gave at the First Anniversary Conference of Conservation 70's in Orlando on July 11, 1970.

The amount of water in the Everglades has always been highly variable. But the point is that we have accented the natural variability— sometimes too wet for too long, or too dry for too long, or simply going from wet to dry or dry to wet much too rapidly. Yo-yo! The long, slow attenuated wets and drys of the past are much compressed in time. As a result we see 15 or 20 species and a National Park which are rare and endangered because the new variability exceeds their ancient adaptability.

But there are symptoms and causes of another kind—those having to do with water quality rather than its quantity or seasonality. In developing modern sewage technology we utilize biological principles fundamental in aquatic environments, say a lake or river, to reduce noxious organic materials to relatively innocuous inorganic nitrates, phosphates, CO_2, etc. We do this in the belief that these will be washed harmlessly downstream. It is a valid assumption too, until we surpass the assimilative capacity of the receiving stream.

The process in a sewage plant copies the breakdown process in a healthy lake. Animal organic wastes are reduced to the same inorganic substances by the microorganisms of decay in the presence of oxygen. The plant life of the lake uses the inorganic products to reconstitute organic materials through photosynthesis, thus recycling the materials back to the animals of the system. The plants, of course, produce oxygen, thus helping to replenish that consumed by the decay organisms.

The sewage plant technology accepts the biological principle of breaking down organic materials, but discharging excessive quantities of nitrate and phosphate into natural waters disregards the remaining portion of the aquatic cycle—the part in which plant life utilizes the inorganics to produce what we started with: organics.

Given a sufficient input of inorganic nutrients, any lake will become over-enriched. It is particularly easy to accomplish this in lakes which are shallow, warm, have lost their marshes, and which have little annual fluctuation.

Excessive input of inorganics will first be evidenced by visible growths of algae, called algal blooms. If repeated and extensive, these are our early-warning symptoms—like the rare and endangered species of animals. If algae are produced too rapidly some results will be:

1. Shading out of rooted aquatic plants by the dense layer of algae.

2. Die-offs of some of the algae itself also through shading.

3. Development of noxious odors, especially in shallows, from the rotting algae.

4. Depletion of oxygen by decaying organic material.

5. An excessive rain of dead organic materials to the bottom, blanketing it with ooze, which destroys vital bottom organisms and fish nesting areas.

6. Diminishing ratios of bass and bluegill populations in favor of gizzard shad as the lake fills with organic material.

The process can be speeded if, in addition to treated effluent, we also add to the lake untreated or improperly treated sewage, cow manure, industrial wastes, phosphates from detergents, and fertilizers leached from farmlands.

We have all of these requirements—the causes—in our Everglades basin and the symptoms are appearing.

In Lake Tohopekaliga in the Kissimmee chain of lakes, a heavy growth of algae occurred beginning about February 1 of 1970. The occurrence of this bloom is certainly an indicator of over-enrichment.

The critical assimilative capacity of the lake for nutrients has been passed and it is responding as we expected. The principal algal species in this bloom is an obnoxious one—Aphanizomenum—for this alga is known to have caused sickness and death to cattle, horses, sheep, hogs, birds, fishes, dogs, and humans from the toxic substances which it produces. Because of the evidences of deteriorating water quality in Lake Toho, the Florida Game and Fresh Water Fish Commission has proposed a drastic draw-down for this lake. Such an action is, I believe, necessary to help counteract the degradation process.

The enrichment problem is not confined to Lake Toho. Farther down the Kissimmee basin several lakes, including Lake Istokpoga and Lake Kissimmee, exhibited extensive algal blooms this year. Observers in the area have noted algal concentrations moving down the channelized lower Kissimmee to Lake Okeechobee. A heavy growth of algae was observed in the northeast part of Okeechobee in March of this year. This material is transported down the Saint Lucie Canal (all of it dies when it reaches salt water), and it adds to the layer of organic ooze which blankets the bottom of the Saint Lucie estuary.

On the south rim of Lake Okeechobee, waters from adjacent farmlands are discharged into the lake. These waters are highly mineralized and are reported to have the poorest quality of those entering Lake Okeechobee. Two fish kills have occurred in the past 3 years in this area—an apparent association with the low quality of the water.

Another symptom of water enrichment (widespread in the canals and lakes of the basin) is the persistent hyacinth, which requires continuing control with sprays or mechanical removal. We might pointedly describe these water quality conditions by paraphrasing the words of Tom Lehrer's song on pollution by saying that if the Aphanizomenum doesn't get you, the hyacinth will.

Another kind of water quality problem is occurring in the channelized Kissimmee and in Lake Okeechobee. Massive amounts of silt—stirred by the dredging of the channel—move down to Okeechobee and have been observed there in a radius of 6 to 8 miles around the mouth of the canal.

These many problems of water quantity and water quality are closely associated with two human activities in the basin. The first human activity involves the supercharge of fertilizing materials into the basin. These now include agricultural fertilizers, many sources of sewage wastes, cow manure, and industrial wastes. They enter the system in too many places to enumerate and the sources—especially human sewage sources—are increasing.

The other kind of human activity is construction work of the flood control project. Reduction of the fluctuation levels of the Kissimmee lakes to less than historic ranges aggravates the enrichment condition. Rapid oxidation of organic materials, which occurs naturally on the shallow bottoms when they are exposed by low lake levels, has been greatly reduced.

Channelization of the lower Kissimmee gives both quantity and quality problems. Drainage of most of the marshes because of the speeded runoff has essentially removed the long, slow flow of Kissimmee waters to Okeechobee—a factor so vital in the ecology of the Everglades. The rapid runoff helps the lake to rise rapidly, sometimes putting it too high for safe control, and forces the discharge of fresh water to the sea—water which the ecosystem needs later to maintain its long, wet period. It is also lost water which man soon will need.

Drainage of the Kissimmee marshes and the loss of marshes around Lake Okeechobee also increase the water quality problems. Marsh vegetation is able to absorb large quantities of fertilizing materials and to convert them beneficially to muck and peat. Much of the fertility which the marshes might have absorbed is now converted into algae in the remaining waters.

Drainage of the marshes has also cost about 50 percent or more of the original waterfowl habitat, plus that of alligators and nesting marsh birds.

We have a host of problems—I have only briefly touched them! No one can at this time delineate the spectrum of corrective measures needed, but I can suggest a few.

We must inventory all input sources of nutrients and correct them. This will involve construction and upgrading of sewage systems and industrial waste treatment systems throughout the basin. Cow manure must be intercepted and hopefully put to some beneficial use. In handling all wastes, maximum recycling of the materials and the water must be the eventual goal.

We must re-flood lake and river marshes throughout the system. This is especially critical in the lower Kissimmee.

We must reestablish the long attenuated flow throughout the system. To do this in the lower Kissimmee will involve drastic alteration of the channeled system. Whether this can be done by impoundments or not, I do not know. Certainly the channelization was a costly mistake—which we shall have to repair sooner or later if we are to continue to supply quality water to the wildlife and human inhabitants of South Florida.

The conservation areas must be fully protected at all times and they should be utilized as regulatory flow routes rather than regarded as reservoirs.

Much of the Big Cypress portion of the basin should be acquired in the public domain—certainly its lower sloughs and ponds—to provide maximum water conservation there.

The southwest Dade area should never be drained.

The wedge of land lying immediately below the east-west portion of Canal C-111 should be acquired and added to Everglades National Park.

A reexamination of the entire ecosystem by ecologists and a variety of natural scientists, engineers, and technicians must be made. This effort will require the services of 50 to 100 persons or more and probably will take three years. All concerned agencies—local, state, and federal—should participate in this massive effort, but it should be headed by a person, *not* in a mission-oriented agency. The products of this effort should be implemented with the same degree of compulsion which the present flood control works have received.

For the need is great. It is the future of much of Florida's salt and freshwater resources—and it is the future of South Florida man, who might himself become a symptom!

THERE IS MORE TO THE GLADES
THAN MEETS THE EYE

Al Volker

Many persons roar at 50 miles an hour through the Everglades, look out across the saw grass marshes and ask, "Is that all there is? " They'd be surprised by all the activity in even a single square yard of what appears to be a deserted landscape, scientists say.

Attracted by the valiant fight to keep alive the unique life network in South Florida, many tourists will be disappointed because they see no alligators or water moccasins. Since they will no doubt report to their friends back home that the Everglades is a wasteland not worth saving, biologists are disturbed.

To biologists the saw grass communities are teeming with life—small life, humble life, foundation stones for the life structure that houses man himself. To the ecologist dealing with life and its relationship to its environment, plants and animals too small to be seen with the unaided eye are as important as gamefish and raccoons.

"Each person has a different way of looking at a natural scene," said Dr. Milton C. Kolipinski, biologist with the United States Geological Survey. "When you know about all those animals out there as you look around, a person like me is filled with awe." He and his associate, Aaron L. Higer, have for years taken twice-monthly samples from ten locations in saw grass marshes of Everglades National Park. Each square yard of marsh is a world in miniature, said Kolipinski. Under normal conditions, various life forms get along well together in a natural balance. Repeated samples with a 5 by 10-foot net, he said, showed average populations of 23.7 small fishes in the daytime and 35.8 at night.

These are fishes that are no more than an inch or two long, including the mosquitofish that likes miniature shrimp, sailfin mollies that feed

Mr. Volker is science editor for the *Miami News*. This chapter appeared in the *Miami News* on April 6, 1970 and is reprinted here by permission of the *Miami News*.

mostly on algae; flagfish, which relish both; and sheepshead minnows, which prefer algae. Other miniature fishes that live in these 50-square foot areas are marsh killfish, least killifishes, and others, as well as tadpoles, freshwater prawn, and insect larvae and adults, principally dragonflies.

But these are all visible dwellers. Under the microscope can be seen many more—the dominant periphyton complex. This is also called the algal mat, growing rapidly on the ground and around plant stems, said Kolipinski and Higer in a recent publication. The mat grows especially thick at the bottom of clear pools. It is composed of billions of microscopic plants such as diatoms and desmids, interlaced filaments and individual cells of algae, microscopic animals, and detritus, or waste. Amphipods, or crustaceans a twenty-fifth of an inch long, feed on the detritus.

Acting upon the algal mat are billions of bacteria, molds, and yeasts. Tiny fishes, tadpoles, insect larvae—principally those of mosquitoes and dragonflies—eat either the microscopic living or dead plants or the microscopic living or dead animals.

The square yard of marsh is, of course, in the river of grass, and the water moves slowly along. Eventually all of these forms of life will reach the brackish water estuaries, the nurseries for infant shrimp and fish. A snail rasps away at one of the kinds of oxygen-producing plants—sedges, such as the spike-rushes; grasses, such as the panic grasses. Numerous spiders construct shining bridges above the shallow, gently-moving waters. A frog hops into the square-yard realm and gulps a small crayfish. Alligators, bigger fish, possums, and wading birds all invade the tiny nation to feed on other citizens and each other.

Nothing going on in the Everglades? You should camp out in those quiet marshes, said Higer. The din will keep you awake—nightbirds and frogs, the calls of animals and the hum of insects. A person sitting quietly for a few moments can see an amazing variety of living things. But the hurrying visitor, too busy to examine a beautiful and fierce little world, sees nothing but the saw grass swaying in the breeze and asks, "Is that all there is?"

ALGAE AND AEROJET

Gene Marine

Nancy Maynard is a graduate biologist at the Marine Institute of the University of Miami. She looks rather as though her life should be dedicated to dinners and dancing at the Beefster, with a Clos Veugeot to accompany the *boeuf charolaise.* In fact, it is dedicated to wading hip-deep in the Florida Everglades, studying the ecology of epiphytic algae.

In her laboratory at the Institute, overlooking that part of Biscayne Bay which is south of the Rickenbacker Causeway and still excruciatingly beautiful, Miss Maynard explained to me that algae (or any other life forms) are "epiphytic" when they live on the surface of other life forms—in this case, on the saw grass that is the most common vegetation of the Everglades. Her studies are done in the southeastern part of Everglades National Park near Barnes Sound, where the water that covers the glades has almost reached an estuarine state—that is, where it is about ready to mix with the salt water of the sea. . . .

Why these particular algae? I asked her curiously. Her answer was disarmingly simple: "Because they won't be there very much longer."

By the time I talked with Nancy Maynard in Florida, I had already had drilled into me by ecologists—Ron Dagon in New York, John Milton and Stanley Cain in Washington, the great Eugene P. Odum in Georgia—the concept of the conservation of genetic information. But it is not all that easy to break old thinking habits, and I found that I had applied the idea mostly to the standard candidates for conservation: the whooping crane and the California condor, the alligator, the cougar. It is more difficult to remember that the same concept applies to the

Mr. Marine is a free-lance writer, a former editor of *Ramparts Magazine.* This chapter was first published as Chapter 3 of *America the Raped* by Gene Marine, Simon and Schuster, New York, 1969, and is reprinted here by permission of Mr. Marine. Copyright © 1969 by Gene Marine.

ebony spleenwort in the New Jersey Pine Barrens, or to ears of corn, or to epiphytic algae. . . .

I had a pretty good idea, too, why the epiphytic algae of the Everglades were expected to disappear, but I asked anyway. For reply, Nancy Maynard asked me, "Do you know about C-111? "

The only C-111 I had ever heard of was an armed forces cargo plane, but I had picked up enough Florida vocabulary to know that it had to be a Corps of Engineers canal. In fact, Nancy Maynard was the fourth person in three days to urge on me a flood-control map of central and southern Florida, showing in garish red and green the existing and proposed network of canals, levees, dams, pumping stations and control centers with which the Engineers are transforming all of the bottom of the state. To anyone who has ever so much as heard the word "ecology," the map is a horror. It is an uncaring and terrifying symbol of the triumph of the Engineers and the rape of America.

The key to the existence of Southern Florida—not only its Miami Beach-Jackie Gleason economic existence, but its ecological existence—is the flow of water. From the central part of the state, water flows into Lake Okeechobee. From there it does not so much flow as seep southward and southwestward, across vast acres of saw grass dotted with higher areas (or "hammocks") that bear shrubs and trees (on these hammocks for centuries lived the Seminoles, feeding on some of the 150-odd species of fish, the dozens of species of birds, living in harmony with deer and alligator, moccasin and panther). Finally, the water flows into Florida Bay, mixing gradually with the salt water of the ocean to form one of the richest estuarine areas in the world. "This tremendous productivity," explains the National Park Service, "is in part dependent upon gradual salinity gradients from fresh to sea water across a broad estuarine belt. The major aquatic species to a degree are abundant because they have free access to whatever proportions of the salt gradient they need at different times in their life cycle."

The shrimp, for instance, which breed in those estuarine waters where fresh water mixes with salt, need an exact proportion of salt in the water—no more, no less—at any given moment in their lives, and it varies from one period in their lives to another. Of course they need other things as well, including the nutrients that come to them in the fresh water; and, as with most life forms, we cannot say with any certainty just what conditions, and in what combinations, are ultimately necessary to their survival. . . . The fluctuation itself in southern

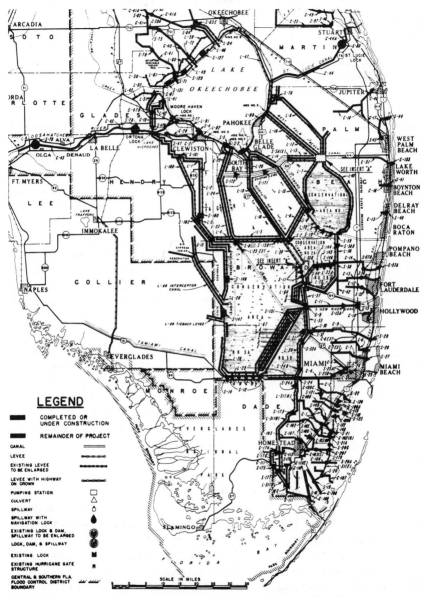

*Central and Southern Florida Flood Control Project. Canals
are shown as heavy lines.*

29

Florida is of a kind that can barely be imagined in the rest of the country. As an example, at the Corkscrew Swamp Sanctuary (in Collier County, Florida, outside the Everglades National Park), M. Philip Kahl, Jr., who was studying the ecology of the wood stork, recorded that in one season, the surface of Saylor Pond grows to two hundred times its smallest area—but its depth increases by only 20 inches.

From the point of view of the casual visitor, this fluctuation makes February a fine time to visit the Everglades; when the water is low, the animals, birds and fish come together in the relatively few wet areas and are easily seen at places like Taylor Slough. From the point of view of some of the wildlife, the fluctuation is essential; some of the birds, for instance, are grope feeders: They simply light in or next to the water and plunge their bills in at random. In low water there is enough food compressed into a small area to last them through the difficult high-water months.

Kahl's scientific prose is not entirely devoted to the wood stork; he also notes in passing what the Engineers have done to the Everglades (only the southern portion of the Everglades is protected in the national park; the rest is open to travel, hunting, airboating—and management). The fertile system described just now is the natural system, but, writes Kahl, it is no more:

> Originally, the Everglades were fed by water overflowing the south rim of Lake Okeechobee, but water-control measures by man, largely within this century, have altered the situation considerably. At present, the overflow from Lake Okeechobee is diverted down drainage controls to the Atlantic Ocean and to the Gulf of Mexico; as a result, the Everglades region now gets most of its water from local rains only.

You don't have to be an expert to know that that's going to foul up the whole Everglades ecosystem.

Actually, the Corps of Engineers is charged by Congress with the responsibility for providing water to the park, whatever else it does—and every year, as Congress pours more money into changing Florida into a sort of Kansas-with-a-seacoast, the legislators are nevertheless careful to keep that provision in the law.

But it works out better on paper than in fact. The water that the Engineers "control" from Lake Okeechobee south is stored under the actual control of something called the Central and Southern Florida Flood Control District ("C&SFFCD" for short), set up in 1949—two years after the national park was established. This means in practice that five unpaid men, meeting once a month, control a project they cannot possibly understand. Of the five men who ran the District in 1966, for instance, one managed his own investments at Kissimmee, one was a real estate operator at Melbourne, one was an agriculturalist at South Bay (much of the Corps operation involves draining the area south of Lake Okeechobee to open it up for agricultural development), one was an insurance man in Coral Gables, and one sold Chevrolets at Fort Pierce.

In 1965, this group and the Corps of Engineers brought down on themselves a little well-earned indignation by holding up water from the drought-ridden Everglades and from the national park until several species of wildlife were endangered and the breeding of others had declined to a point from which recovery is still uncertain. In the meantime, in the Everglades north of the park, deer which would normally have retreated slowly to high ground as the water rose were, instead, wandering all over the area. Finally, as indignation grew, the District agreed to release water to the park and to the glades—and released it in one great rush, drowning thousands of deer.

Obviously, to talk about "how much water the Everglades get" in terms of acre-feet per year is nonsense. The Everglades constitute one of the most delicately balanced ecological mechanisms found anywhere in the world. . . .

How delicately the Everglades life depends on the water situation is demonstrated by Kahl's study of the wood stork. When the water drops to a certain level every year, the wood stork lays eggs. It doesn't matter what day it is, or how long the days are, or what the temperature is, or how much light there is: When the water level hits that point, that's it. And it isn't just the amount of water, either; if rain made up the difference for all the water drained off by the Engineers, it still wouldn't help the wood stork. For one thing, there are nutrients in the natural flow water (and of course nobody knows what nutrients and nobody knows how they are used in the delicate ecosystem), and there are almost certainly other elements that affect the oxidation of organic soils, the trends in plant succession, and a number of other factors. To complicate matters, water used first for agriculture is likely to contain pesticide residues.

The wood stork knows whether the water is natural or not. North of the national park is an east-west highway, the Tamiami Trail, beneath which the Everglades water flows through a series of culverts; this is one of the places at which water flow is regularly measured. Park officials have discovered that whenever the water flow through the Tamiami Trail is 300,000 acre-feet or more per year, the wood stork successfully nests; whenever the water flow falls below 225,000 acre-feet, the nesting fails. Rain doesn't make up for it, no matter how much there is; the water has to flow in from the north in the normal fashion.

The park, then, is slowly dying, thanks to the Engineers. Outside the office window of Superintendent Allin, just inside the park boundary near Homestead, I saw woody brush dominating a landscape that should have been mostly saw grass and a few hammocks. It is what happens when year after year is dry, and it will take years—if, indeed, it can ever be done at all—to restore the area to its "natural" form.

In nature, of course, wildfire would be a major ecological factor acting toward restoration, and would serve also the function of decomposing much of the organic material for reuse. During the drought of 1967, nearly a million acres of brush and timberland burned in southern Florida, most of it outside the park. Although the natural role of fire is little understood by the general public, it is well understood by ecologists. Still, Park Service policy is against even controlled burning, and of course wildfire cannot be allowed to burn uncontrolled when there is always a minimum of three or four thousand visitors in the park.

"I'd like to burn it," Allin admitted to me, "but I'd like even more to see the park get the water it would naturally get."

On the garish Corps of Engineers map that Nancy Maynard pressed into my hand, I found a short red line, running a few miles northwest from Barnes Sound and crossing U.S. Highway 1. On that master plan for billion-dollar chaos, the one tiny line is inconspicuous enough, but it's the one she wanted me to see. It is labeled "C-111."

C-111 is a canal that already exists, although at the moment it has a "plug" in it. The plug was supposed to be pulled a few weeks after I was there, but the National Audubon Society managed to get a court order holding up the procedure. The situation is still unresolved. If it were pulled, it would mean serious enough damage if only Nancy Maynard's epiphytic algae are destroyed—the algae whose ecological role, possibly a crucial one, she and her co-workers are only now trying to determine. But the destruction is, in fact, likely to be far more dramatic.

C-111 has two avowed purposes. One of them is that ubiquitous excuse for anything the Engineers want to do: flood control. The canal will take the fresh water that flows "overland" in a southwesterly direction into the park and divert it into Barnes Sound—thus changing, when and if it works, the salinity of the sound and probably of whole sections of Florida Bay. When there isn't fresh water to divert, the salt water of the sound will come up the canal—and change salinity in the other direction.

In addition, if there is salt water in the canal, as there will be during times of drought, then a hurricane or even a high wind from the southeast is almost certain to blow a lot of that salt water over the canal's banks and into the Everglades, where it will flow south and southwest—salt and all—and damage the whole ecology of the area. In a way, this is the bitterest irony of all; the Corps of Engineers' first excuse for messing with southern Florida was that hurricane winds would sometimes blow water out of Lake Okeechobee, flooding surrounding lands.

The second purpose of C-111 is to provide a channel for barge transportation to a plant operated by the Aerojet-General Company. C-111 is openly called "the Aerojet canal," and true or not, it is widely believed that Aerojet's tremendous political influence as a prime defense contractor bolsters the Engineers' determination to ignore the protests of the Park Service and virtually everyone else about the opening of the canal. . . .

Just about all the fish in the Everglades require just the right depth and duration of water, and the right salt content, in order to feed and to reproduce. A lot of them go back and forth from fresh to estuarine water, staying where the salt gradient is just right. A lot more live in estuarine water all the time.

Even if conserving genetic information were not of overriding importance, Floridians will be cutting off not only their noses but their ears, hands and feet if they don't stop the Engineers pretty soon. As long ago as 1964, the scientists who made the study just mentioned reported that "Florida Bay . . . shows increasingly frequent and long-sustained periods of super-salinity," and added:

Salinities of 70 parts per thousand, twice that of seawater, are already frequently encountered. This can be serious biologically; salinities this high are lethal to the eggs and young of nearly all marine species, and the adults of only a few species can tolerate such salinity.

Think about that—especially if you live in, or like to visit, Florida. Because those "marine species" that will all die off if the Engineers are not stopped include, among a lot of others, the menhaden—which supports by far the greatest fishery of the United States; the black mullet, which supports the largest food-fish landings in Florida; the spotted sea trout, which Florida fishermen love so well; the snook; the tarpon; blue crabs; stone crabs; oysters; and the extremely valuable pink shrimp, worth millions of dollars a year commercially to Florida and vital as a food for many fish besides.

There is no way around this. It is possible, I suppose, that the citizens of Florida don't care any more than anybody else does about the conservation of genetic information. It is even possible that they are willing to let the Engineers destroy millions of dollars worth of industry and tourism. For any such determined Florida promoters, I offer one more long-range warning from Dr. Odum, who suggests that too much drainage "would not only ruin the area as a wildlife paradise but would also be risky in that salt water might then intrude into the underground water supply needed by the large coastal cities."

You can already get salt water out of the kitchen faucet, some days, in Atlantic City, New Jersey. Why not Miami?

But the Engineers intend to go on, and this year it's C-111. The "hydrologic change" caused by that one little canal, itself only about 7 miles long, will spread over at least 200 square miles. Within those 200 square miles are 60 percent of the park's roseate spoonbills, 25 percent of the great white herons, 15 percent of the American eagles and 95 percent of the dwindling numbers of crocodiles (not alligators)—among other species. All of these birds and animals are already in the "rare and endangered" classification.

Of course the Park Service has complained. The Engineers, however, have an answer. We'll pull the plug, the Corps has said, "to see what damages would occur and thereby justify the Service's claim that a plug is necessary"! If ever there was an Engineer's answer, that's it. The Park Service treats it with the contempt it deserves:

First, irreparable damage might well occur within a matter of hours; second, it may well be that many of the damages which could occur would not be obvious even with close surveillance. Very likely such changes could be subtle, long-term biological changes which in their ultimacy would be devastating, but not readily observable in the early stages of their unalterable course.

The Engineers couldn't care less about the roseate spoonbill, much less the epiphytic algae. In fact—just so they get to build something, and Aerojet gets its barge access to the sea—they couldn't care less about the Everglades, indescribably beautiful and unique as they are, and constituting as they do the only national park that was created specifically to preserve an ecosystem. . . .

Even the wholesale havoc of C-111 isn't enough for the Engineers. Now they're talking about moving over to the other coast to dam the rivers, streams and sloughs of the Shark River and Whitewater Bay drainages, and about building a couple of hundred or thousand "low-head dams" throughout the interior of Everglades National Park itself.

There is no stopping the engineering mentality. We can only try to stop the Engineers.

THE EVERGLADES, THE JETPORT,
AND THE FUTURE

Joe Browder

The hazards of the Everglades have changed somewhat since they were dramatized in the theme song of a television series a few years ago. A musical lament for life in the Glades today would have to say "if the airplanes don't get you then the oil well will." Just north of Everglades National Park, high above the receding waters of the Big Cypress Swamp, jetliners are using airspace once reserved for wood storks. In the same watershed, between the jetport and the Park, oil-drilling crews are planning to force steel through the Everglades earth and to try to find still another reason to destroy the land.

Since its establishment in 1947, Everglades National Park has been compromised geographically, biologically, and politically. But now the Everglades may have a chance, after all. President Nixon has emphatically decided against completion of the Big Cypress jetport. If the decision is enforced, it will be the first real victory in the continuing battle to protect the Park.

President Nixon's determination to relocate the airport could mean the beginning of a new national policy to truly preserve the Everglades. Past crises, such as the conflict over flood control interference with the Everglades water supply, have invariably led to accommodations against the best interests of the National Park. The Corps of Engineers and its economic and political constituents usually get what they want, regardless of the consequences to the Park. But this time, the message from the White House was clear: move the airport, and never mind the cost in either dollars or discomfort to those who supported the ill-conceived project.

Mr. Browder was Southeast Regional Director for the National Audubon Society and led the fight to relocate the Everglades jetport. He is currently the Washington Director of Friends of the Earth, an environmental lobbying organization. This chapter was first published in the March 1970 issue of *Audubon Magazine* and is reprinted here by permission of the National Audubon Society.

Of course, the jetport has not yet been moved. The Dade County Port Authority has agreed to do so, if and when the federal government comes up with another airport site and training runway at no cost to the Port Authority. This means the United States will foot the $13,000,000 bill for correcting the Port Authority's mistake. It will be a small price to pay, and a fair one, because local authorities and airline industry executives who chose the Big Cypress site did so with the approval of the Federal Aviation Administration and without any effective opposition from former Interior Secretary Stewart L. Udall.

The Port Authority, the State of Florida, and the United States government have signed a contract permitting temporary use of the existing runway until a new site is developed. The Port Authority has promised to diligently search for a new location—but as long as the jets are using the Big Cypress airport, some men will continue to work for its full development. Members of the Dade County Port Authority have said privately that those who love the Everglades are naive—that no issue can capture public attention forever, so that if the search for an alternate site can be prolonged, the climate in Washington will eventually change and the Port Authority will be able to turn the training runway into the world's largest commercial airport.

President Nixon could not be stronger in his opposition to the Everglades jetport. We believe that the Dade County politicians are themselves naive to think that this or any administration would sacrifice Everglades National Park to such an obvious threat. But the landmark nature of the jetport decision could be a detriment to the Park, if it detracts from the real issue—the preservation and good management of the Everglades watershed.

Three decades ago, when much of the Big Cypress watershed was included in the National Park's proposed boundaries, the swamp was held by a handful of owners. When the final Park boundary was drawn, the line had been shifted to exclude the Big Cypress. In the past few years, this land has been carved into more than 30,000 parcels—most of them belonging to absentee owners who have never seen their soggy piece of Florida real estate. Since the traditional battle for the Everglades has been over control of the waters of the river of grass, the importance of the Big Cypress Swamp was largely ignored until the jetport controversy. The Tamiami Trail and Alligator Alley trace westward from Miami and Fort Lauderdale through saw grass and cypress, then reach civilization again in the Naples area. The saw grass glades, nearest to the booming east coast cities, have long been drained, diked, and otherwise manipulated. But, fortunately, southwest Florida has not yet been transformed by such feverish development as the Palm Beach-Miami gold coast. The cypress country is still relatively free from destructive human intrusion. Men drive through it, or hunt and fish in it, without significantly interfering with the flow of water south into the National Park.

This water flow is vital to the Park and to the wilderness north of the Park boundaries. But men who bought up that wilderness by the acre have visions of selling it by the front foot, and the water is in their way. The jetport stirred a development frenzy that can only be satisfied if the cypress country is drained. With visions of dollar signs still in their eyes, would-be developers are not giving up just because the jetport may be moved. Between the jetport site and the National Park, speculators plan to drain more than 50 square miles of privately owned Everglades, including some inholdings within the Park boundaries. The land contains Gum Slough, one of the principal natural basins that distributes water into the Park from the cypress country to the north. The National Audubon Society and other property owners in the area have gone to court to try to stop the drainage project, and the United States government has petitioned to intervene in the case to help protect the Park. But the Gum Slough proposal seems modest compared to other drainage schemes developing in the Big Cypress.

Roughly a half-million acres of the Big Cypress needs to be preserved in order to protect the Park's water supply. Landowners say the entire area should be drained—at public expense. Property owners are lobbying for an extensive network of canals and other water-control structures, roads, and other "improvements" designed to dry up the Big Cypress and turn it into a promoters' paradise.

It would cost the American taxpayers more to let speculators develop the Big Cypress than it would to buy the whole area and preserve it. Nearly $200,000,000 has been spent on the half-completed drainage and flood control system that serves central and southeast Florida. If the Big Cypress is not purchased and preserved, hundreds of millions of tax dollars will be spent on similar land reclamation projects in southwest Florida—and the Big Cypress and Everglades National Park will be lost. Drainage of the Big Cypress would have a political and economic impact far beyond the boundaries of the swamp. Just as the saw grass glades purify and replenish the freshwater supply for southeast Florida, the Big Cypress serves as a water resource for communities on the southwest coast. If the Big Cypress were to be drained and developed, southwest Florida would destroy its own watershed while increasing the demand for water. This would force the expanding populations of Naples and Fort Myers to turn to a flood control system already unable to meet the water demands of southeast Florida.

The State of Florida's inability to wisely manage its water resources puts Everglades National Park, and all current water users, in an untenable position. A finite supply cannot satisfy an infinite demand, yet the state refuses to recognize that there is only so much water to go around. Drought is a part of the natural Everglades cycle, and the National Park expects to face dry years. But unless the state recognizes Everglades National Park as a legitimate water user, the Park's share of the water will continually diminish as new users make demands on the system. Current urban and agricultural water users who view the Everglades as a competitor will soon learn that the Park's needs are small compared to the demands of the millions of persons who could move to Florida in the next few years.

And now, oil wells. Oil exploration in the Everglades is nothing new. Oil fever prompted some Florida politicians to try to prevent the establishment of the National Park more than twenty years ago. Perhaps it is just as well that drilling rigs will rise again in the Glades. They serve to remind us that the jetport issue was, after all, only another in the series of annual Everglades crises, and that nothing has been done to correct the system that produces the crises.

The Big Cypress Swamp, the last source of free-flowing water for the Everglades, is about to be drained, drilled, and developed. The State of Florida refuses to recognize that the National Park has just as much right to water as a Lake Okeechobee celery farm. The entire question of water quality is a painful embarrassment to the state, and pollution presents a danger to the Park that may outweigh the threat of an outright water shortage. Again, the magnitude of President Nixon's decision on the jetport offers hope that the long-range problems of the Park will be solved.

The Everglades is life itself—a unique example of the process responsible for all being: energy from the sun, captured and converted by the most fundamental plant and animal forms; matter and life moving through air and water, cycled through a web of complex and interrelated systems. We are a part of this world of the Everglades; in damaging it we endanger our own community. Humans in the coastal cities of Florida are as dependent on the flow of energy, water, and life through the Everglades as are the birds and alligators that inhabit the saw grass and cypress, or the fish and shrimp we harvest offshore.

If we do not make the commitments necessary to assure the survival of the Everglades, we will lose more than a great National Park. If man will not live with a living Everglades, he will have to find a new definition for humanity. If man cannot live with a living Everglades, he may be incapable of continuing success as a species. If man can choose to try and save the Everglades, perhaps he can save himself as well.

THE POPULATION EXPLOSION
IN DADE COUNTY

E. R. Rich

If you live in the far north reaches of Dade County and are frustrated by the daily drive through bumper-to-bumper traffic, you can look forward to a doubled population in your area in the next ten years.

If you live in southwest Dade County and are concerned with the present crowded condition of the schools, be glad that your children will be out of elementary school ten years from now when there will be half again as many children in your area.

Consider the rush hour traffic on Bird Road and try to imagine twice as many people living at its western end. Or consider nearly a 50 percent increase in the Sunday afternoon crowds trying to get to and from Key Biscayne for an afternoon of Fun in the Sun.

We can look forward to this because Dade County is adding to its population at the rate of over 120 people per day. As many people as live in the city of Coral Gables are being added every year. Perhaps we should be delighted at all these new taxpayers coming to share our burden—coming to contribute to the economy. But perhaps we should be ready to panic because these new arrivals are competitors for our air—our land—our water—even our sunshine. Let us consider the demands which they will make and the effect of these demands on the quality of life here in the Sun and Fun Capital of the World.

Housing will be needed—over 16,000 new units per year. We will bulldoze away the pine woods and convert the farm lands from their economic productivity. We will pump more of the good sweet water and then worry about how to handle it when it is turned into sewerage. There is a silver lining to this cloud—some land speculators will be able to make a profit of inflated dollars.

These new neighbors will want to drive their cars—over 16,000 of

Dr. Rich is professor of zoology in the Department of Biology at the University of Miami, where he teaches courses on population biology.

them. We can't put more streets in the developed areas, but we might be able to tear up and widen the existing ones so that they can carry more lanes bumper-to-bumper. This has a silver lining too. We will be able to build more gas stations and collect more gas tax.

Our new friends will have children—not so many as their predecessors who came in the fifties, but maybe of the added 43,000 some 15,000 will be children and about 9,000 of them in school. To take care of schooling, we must build four new elementary schools each year, one additional junior high school every year, and another senior high school every other year.

To properly provide for our population increase, we will need a new sewerage treatment plant and several new fire stations. In a year we can expect our new fellow citizens to be involved as victims or perpetrators of over 800 crimes. About 85 of their autos will be stolen. To cope with this criminal activity, we will have to spend $1,000 per day.

Some of our new friends may get sick. We can expect 125 of them to need hospitalization in a mental institution. In any given year, of this group of 43,000, 600 will spend over 57,000 days in a hospital. To provide this service, we need an additional 387-bed hospital.

These demands are made by the people added in one year. The next year there will be a like number and the year after that a like number. It won't take long before South Florida is no longer recognizable as the land of good living.

Some will read these projections and be overjoyed, but a fool's delight is short-lived. The taxpayer who expects relief will be disappointed. The Chamber of Commerce type who thinks "growth is good" will soon learn worse. For a growing regional economy to prosper, there must be an increasing net flow of money into the region. Passing money from hand to hand does not increase the wealth of the community. One way to make money is for local people to sell to outsiders a product which is locally produced. Dade County's agriculture does this now and it is an economic asset. But the more tract houses and apartment buildings we put up in the tomato fields, the less our agriculture can contribute to the economy. We have little mineral wealth which is locally owned that we can mine and sell, so there is no opportunity here.

Another way to make money is to have outsiders bring their money here and spend it. The tourist industry is most valuable in this sense, but it cannot be expected to retain its allure when the beaches are polluted and the coastline becomes wall-to-wall high-rise apartments and hotels around a cesspool bay. Service industries like the airlines represent outside dollars obtained by the skilled labor of local people. But in the jet age Miami loses much of its attractiveness as a transportation center. It lacks the continental advantages of Atlanta and even many of the South American carriers are minimizing their Miami activities. Perhaps South Florida could make it as a commercial center. But Miami is the center of nothing. A business which can tie to the rest of the country by electronic communication can center its activities here. We can shuffle the papers. But if the ownership isn't here, the profits go away. Manufacturing is nice if we don't have to import expensive raw materials and if we can sell very expensive products to people in other places. Here too, we are off the main path.

Off the main path—perhaps this is the reason many of us are in South Florida. Perhaps we choose to live in a place where the economy is a bit slower. We want to enjoy a life that is good without trying to mimic Manhattan. Perhaps we would like to see agriculture and tourism as major industries and to enjoy the clean world that is good for farming and attractive to tourists. A place which is so wonderfully endowed with beauty and opportunity for good living is worth keeping. Unless we are willing to plan for the future with due consideration for the environmental assets, there will be little of value for future generations of Floridians and tourists.

POPULATION CONTROL IN SOUTH FLORIDA

Joyce Tarnow

There are a great many reasons why population growth in South Florida and particularly in Dade County should be controlled *now*. The most obvious reason is the ability to provide adequate services to the present one-and-a-quarter million Dade Countians in the areas of sewage treatment, garbage collection, mass transit, public school facilities, and fire and police protection. Another reason is the lack of sufficient parks and beaches for recreation, while the opportunity to add to these grows slimmer as more "development" crowds the available land. The most crucial reason, however, and the one that will ultimately force a population limit upon us, is the decreasing supply of available fresh water.

A growing number of political leaders and citizens in Dade County have begun to advocate the necessity for limiting population growth. North Bay Village, with the help of the Metropolitan Dade County Planning Department, has drawn up a comprehensive plan to provide a land-use pattern and development standard that will be incorporated into the zoning regulations to insure orderly development and redevelopment of its 123 acres.

In seeking to achieve growth consistent with efficient traffic circulation and adequate municipal services, with transition areas from low to high intensity residential land use, and with minimum requirements for landscaped areas, it was determined that no more than 9,145 people could be accommodated in the village at full development.

On July 21, 1970 the Metropolitan Dade County Commission established still another landmark decision when it unanimously passed Commissioner Earl Starnes' motion that a population maximum of 150,000 be set on the South Bay Study area.

Mrs. Tarnow is an ardent conservationist and is co-director of the Miami Chapter of Zero Population Growth, Inc.

"I think it is high time that we began to reach some population controls," Starnes said. "I don't think we can continue the planning process in response to population. . . . We have to begin to say, as a matter of public policy, that population growth is from now on going to be controlled in Dade County under what rational and lawful means are at our disposal."

The fact that a great number of Dade's citizens agree with the philosophy expressed by Commissioner Starnes was evidenced by the large turnouts of protesters at zoning and commission hearings of development plans in this area submitted by the Saga Corporation. Conservation groups were joined by homeowners' and civic associations, by students, and by unaligned, concerned individuals. One spokesman after another voiced their opposition to the net results of extensive development. They opposed the meagerness of tax income as compared to required public expenditures and to the added negative effects of heavier congestion of roads and recreational facilities by people and vehicles. They did not want increased air pollution from chimneys and exhaust pipes, further deterioration of water quality through inadequate sewage facilities and treatment, nor the additional strain on available fresh water, electrical power supply, trash removal, phone service, and public building funds.

Secondly, they opposed the loss of positive effects rendered by open space—absorption of rainwater into the water table, plant materials to add oxygen to the atmosphere and agricultural products for the table. They opposed the loss of shoreline mangrove areas which serve as nurseries of marine and bird life. One after another the people spoke for quality in the lives of those who are already living here.

While there is still much to debate on what limits should be set on population in Dade County and South Florida, the need to set them is clearly evident. What remains to be determined is how.

Both North Bay Village leaders and Metro's Vice-Mayor Hardy Matheson feel that limiting the number of housing units available through zoning is the most effective tool at hand. Commissioner Starnes would add to this approach the need to discourage migration as well as the need for cooperation from the courts in upholding toughened zoning curbs on development. He also calls for a federal government policy to stop population growth.

While all of these methods move in the right direction they fail to go far enough to protect the quality of life Dade Countians are demanding.

Curbing the number of housing units available is an essential beginning, but without supporting policies, it cannot succeed. Since cutting the supply without reducing the demand would drive up the cost of housing, only the wealthier citizens could afford to compete. However, if a system of issuing a fixed number of housing licenses to present citizens were to be worked out whereby only such licensed persons would be eligible to purchase or to rent housing units, supply and demand would tend to balance out. Some such system would be a necessity.

Regarding the discouragement of migration from other states and other nations, we would again defeat our purpose if we did not also move to halt our own natural increase by adopting a replacement-only policy for future families. The two-child family would eventually stabilize the population at a fixed range once migration was stemmed.

There is an inherent weakness, too, in zoning solutions alone, particularly with regard to undeveloped tracts. Strong zoning ordinances too often fall victim to changes in governmental administrations and to appeals for variances. A more effective safeguard to maintain agricultural lands as agricultural lands and to retain open spaces for the enjoyment and benefit of all is to put them into public ownership with any change in usage to be made only by a referendum in which two-thirds of the people grant approval.

Although these proposals sound drastic to some segments of the populace, they represent new attitudes that are rapidly spreading and gaining strength among those citizens who see drastic changes taking place in their neighborhoods and in the beauty of the environment that made South Florida a desirable place to live. They are totaling up the score-sheets of economic advantage on the one side and human and economic disadvantage on the other. Their arithmetic indicates population controls as the only answer.

THE SOLUTION TO POLLUTION

Ross McCluney

Someone once said: "The solution to pollution is dilution! " In most cases this is quite true. The idea is that if we can just spread the offending pollutant uniformly over a large enough area, it will be dispersed and diluted to a relatively harmless concentration. Like most "pat" answers, this one has its problems. Firstly, you have to make sure you have a large enough area available to accomplish the desired dilution. This is not always easy. If you are planning to dump a waste chemical into a nearby pond you may find that the pond is too small to safely absorb the amount of chemical you plan to dump. For some pollutants the whole ocean is not a big enough place. We presently have a nuclear test ban treaty because the whole world is not large enough to adequately dilute the radioactive wastes resulting from the atmospheric testing of nuclear bombs.

Secondly, you have to provide the physical means (equipment) for proper distribution of the pollutant. You have to be careful not to let it contact the most susceptible portions of the environment while it is still in a concentrated form.

This is one of the most technically difficult aspects of the problem and requires the use of some non-susceptible medium, or intermediate reservoir, within which the dilution can be accomplished before the pollutant is released to the environment. Until we can find economically acceptable methods for rocketing our unwanted (and non-recyclable) pollutants to the sun, we on earth will have to learn to solve these problems.

Another fascinating problem that has recently been found to creep into the picture is something called "biological magnification." It has been found that living organisms have the ability to reconcentrate (or magnify) certain pollutants in their bodies. Even very dilute and harmless concentrations of certain pollutants, like DDT, can become very concentrated in the tissues of certain animals.

The process can be continued up the food chain, producing larger and larger concentrations of the pollutant with each step. This process is thought to be responsible, for example, for the disappearance of the pelican from the Louisiana, Texas, and California coasts.

Thus dilution is not the sole solution to our pollution problems. In many cases, we will simply have to find a way of eliminating the practices that produce "undilutable" pollutants. We must then search for environmentally acceptable alternatives to the previous practices. If they cannot be found, we must be prepared to abandon them completely.

In the case of DDT, there appear to be a number of suitable alternatives to its use. The mosquito can be controlled by several other kinds of pesticides, which break down into relatively harmless substances after a few hours of exposure to the elements. DDT can be replaced in agriculture by a variety of techniques such as organic farming and less-offensive DDT substitutes. The only disadvantage with these alternatives is that they have to be applied more frequently and result in greater costs of operation. The result of a total DDT ban would not be (as some people would have us believe) a massive epidemic of malaria. It would simply be an increase in the cost of mosquito control. Or it would be a slight increase in the cost of raising crops.

Waste heat is an inevitable product of the generation of electricity by available nonhydroelectric means. In the sense that this waste heat can destroy portions of the environment and upset the ecological balance of a region, it is a pollutant. The solution to thermal pollution *is* dilution. In the first place, thermal pollution is not subject to biological magnification. Once diluted it *stays* diluted. In the second place, Professor Claes Rooth of the Rosenstiel School of Marine and Atmospheric Sciences of the University of Miami has done some calculations which show that the whole earth's surface, and its atmosphere, is a large enough place to hold all our thermal wastes without damaging the environment, if they are sufficiently dispersed.

Apart from air pollution from the furnaces of conventional electrical power stations, and pollution by radioactive wastes from nuclear generating facilities, our main problem seems to be in properly

48

spreading our waste heat over a sufficiently large area so that it will not harm the environment.

In the case of the Turkey Point generating station of the Florida Power and Light Company, present plans are to spread the waste heat produced by the new nuclear generators over a relatively large area of lower Biscayne Bay and Card Sound. If the engineering designs for the expanded facility fail to produce sufficient dispersal of the waste heat, it will be too concentrated, too hot, in some places, and significant environmental damage can result. Even if this does not occur, there is another insidious problem that can sneak in to foul things up.

It was said earlier that one must be careful not to let the pollutant (waste heat in this case) contact the most susceptible portions of the environment while it is still in a concentrated form. The waste heat generated at Turkey Point is released to the environment by first drawing bay water into the generating station, heating it up, and then sending it back into the bay (at a different location) to be dispersed. Since the bay water used in the process contains numerous tiny plants and animals which are vital components of the bay ecosystem, this water and the organisms it transports must be considered "susceptible" to environmental degradation. Thus, if the waste heat is put into this water in too concentrated a form, that is, if the water passing through the cooling tubes is allowed to get too hot, then significant environmental destruction can follow.

We are here faced with the possibility that the bay water might become at least partially sterilized in its passage through the heating tubes. Considering the large amount of water which will be flowing through this system, large-scale ecological disruption in Biscayne Bay and Card Sound is a very real possibility. This is so even if the subsequent dispersal and dilution of the heated water is successful and undamaging in itself.

The engineers involved in this project must find a way to produce the desired dilution without harming any of the plants and animals that live in the water which passes through the generators. Otherwise they will have to find some other way of getting rid of the waste heat, perhaps without putting it into the bay at all. Dry cooling towers might be a feasible possibility. The atmosphere is probably less susceptible to these heat wastes than is the bay, and it would probably be much easier to accomplish the needed dilution if the heat were to be put directly into the air. As usual, such solutions will very likely cost more money but they can save the bay for recreational use.

Again, the problem boils down to one of balancing economic costs against the costs of environmental destruction. Environmental protection and low business costs seldom go together. If we really want to protect the environment, we must be willing to pay the price.

WATER POLLUTION PROBLEMS
IN DADE COUNTY

Peter P. Baljet

Dade County has water pollution problems. Its waters are dangerously infested with harmful microorganisms and are practically not
suitable for swimming. Many other harmful substances pour into Dade's
waters on a daily basis and continue the present trend of degradation.

There is no question that the 89 sewage treatment plants discharging
some 35 million gallons per day into the canal system, 110 million
gallons per day into the Atlantic Ocean, and some 1.4 million gallons
per day into drainfields have substantially contributed to the pollution.
Most of these plants produced unsatisfactory treatment even in earlier
days.

When excessive sewage is present in a canal, a heavy demand for
oxygen is placed on the stream. This is called biochemical oxygen
demand, or BOD, and is one of the things measured by pollution
control officers to indicate whether or not a body of water is polluted.
If the subject stream is fast flowing, it can at least flush these
deleterious substances into the ocean where they may be dispersed. But
in Dade County, the streams are more or less standing bodies of water,
like lagoons, in a manner of speaking. The waste dumped into them by
sewage treatment plants has thus piled up over the years and is the
cause of the present severity of our pollution crisis.

The picture is such that in actuality, the canals cannot accept one
additional pound of waste, *no matter how good the treatment.* Even
so-called tertiary, or three-step, treatment will not totally remove a
waste loading, and is thus still not good enough. Other measures must
therefore be found to rejuvenate our waters and bring them back to
life.

There is, in the writer's opinion, just one method that can do the

Mr. Baljet served as director of the engineering section of the Dade County
Health Department and was recently appointed Dade County Pollution Control
Officer. He holds an M.S. degree in Civil Engineering from the University of Miami.

job. This method would involve the removal of all existing sewage wastes from the bottoms of the canals and the collection of sewage treatment plant effluents with major transmission mains. These effluents would then be transported by the mains to some other location. One such destination could be an advanced waste-water renovation plant. The effluent from the facility would be so pure that it could be used for drinking and other re-use purposes, such as irrigation of lawns and crops. Another destination could be the Atlantic Ocean, or, in particular, the Gulf Stream.

Perhaps it would be wise to bisect the county at some north-south line. East of this line, highly saline sewage would justifiably be discharged, following appropriate treatment, into the Gulf Stream. The high saline character of the sewage, generated in the mid-eastern section of Dade County (or, rather, the old City of Miami), is caused by excessive infiltration of saline groundwater into old sewage collection lines. This saline water is the result of an intrusion of salt water from the ocean, penetrating inland into the normally fresh water under-ground. It is thus quite logical to simply send waste waters from this area to the ocean. The logic of this approach is based on two facts: (1) The high cost of treating saline sewage, and (2) the waste water in question is more closely identical with the ocean water to which it is destined. West of the imaginary line mentioned above, the renovated sewage would be put back into the ground water, to recharge the Biscayne aquifer, our main source of drinking water.

Poorly treated sewage effluents are the major sources of our problems. A secondary problem is that of septic tanks, underground containers of sewage whose effluent seeps directly into the ground water and poses the threat of contamination of our drinking water. A septic tank is simply a rectangular underground container which retains sewage for some 12 to 24 hours. In this time the suspended solids of the sewage settle out. The tank is simple to construct and requires little care. However, it does not purify sewage. The tank effluent contains disease bacteria and is septic and subject to decomposition with the formation of foul-smelling, incompletely oxidized products.

Some 53 percent of the Dade County populace uses septic tanks. In 1966, the quantity of this poorly-treated effluent rose to over 55 million gallons. Thomas Jackivicz, in his graduate studies at the University of Miami, found that the presence of septic tanks adjacent to waterways is accompanied by significantly high levels of eutrophicants

52

in those waterways. Eutrophicants are mineral nutrients which cause eutrophication or enrichment when introduced into water. They stimulate the growth of algae and other water plants, which use up all the oxygen in the water, leaving little for other organisms.

Septic tanks must go! From a public health standpoint and from the standpoint of pollution control, it is imperative that septic tanks be replaced by sanitary sewer facilities. Realizing that in the suburban areas remote from sewage transmission lines, septic tanks are the solitary system available for the handling of sewage, the writer recognizes that their use could be accepted on an interim basis, provided sufficient area is available around each septic tank in order to insure proper public health protection.

Dade County officials faced with the problems described above are working on revitalizing a sewage master plan for Dade County. It is expected that a proper cleanup job would cost some $1 billion. This cost will have to be carried by us, the citizenry, in conjunction with county, state, and federal funds. The recently passed Amendment 4 to the Florida constitution and the hoped-for enactment of the amendment by the state legislature could result in a cost scheme whereby the county would have to come up with some 25 percent of the cost, with 75 percent being paid by the state and federal governments.

Money, as always, is the key issue. But the answers are available, and implementation is around the corner. Until now, we have been a most destructive and consumptive population; we must now turn this around and learn the art of recycling and re-use!

Since the writer is an engineer, he ends his discussion with the following excerpt from the address of Sir Peter Madawar, the president of the British Association for the Advancement of Science, given at the Association's 1969 meeting:

There is a tendency, even a perverse willingness, to suppose that the despoliation sometimes produced by technology is an inevitable and irremediable process, a trampling down of Nature by the big machine. . . it is nothing of the kind. The deterioration of the environment produced by technology is a technological problem for which technology has found, is finding, and will continue to find solutions.

AIR POLLUTION PROBLEMS
IN SOUTH FLORIDA

Ross McCluney

It is often said that Miami doesn't really have an air pollution problem. By comparison with New York, Chicago, and Los Angeles, for example, South Floridians live in a paradise of abundant clean air. However, by comparison with other parts of the country, places relatively remote from large metropolitan areas, the air in much of South Florida is filled with poisonous gases and other pollutants which can aggravate lung ailments and hasten death for the elderly. For Miami (and South Florida) *does* have an air pollution problem.

The Processes of Air Pollution

The products of combustion become the major pollutants in South Florida's atmosphere. There is, to be sure, a limited amount of vaporized material, such as evaporated gasoline, and dust-like solid particles present, but the products of combustion are the most prevalent.

Combustion takes place in furnaces used to generate electricity, it occurs in incinerators used to burn garbage, and it is the power-producing process which takes place in automobile engines, jet engines, and steam engines. The explosive type of combustion which occurs in the internal combustion engine used to power automobiles is very inefficient and therefore gives off many more harmful pollutants than the relatively efficient combustion in a steam engine.

It is obvious from the available data that air pollution has been steadily increasing since 1966 and is approaching dangerous levels. One doesn't really need a lot of numbers to see that South Florida has an air pollution problem. Let me suggest several ways in which the average citizen can detect air pollution. The first is for people with access to a boat. In this case, you simply cruise out into the Gulf Stream (or into the middle of Biscayne Bay), preferably early in the morning. As the level of automobile traffic increases during early morning rush hours on a clear day, one can see a dirty-looking, yellow-brown haze creep up above the horizon over the portions of the coast having the highest population densities. If the observer is sufficiently far off shore he can see two domes of brown haze, one over Miami and another over Fort Lauderdale. According to Dr. Howard Gordon of the School of Marine and Atmospheric Sciences of the University of Miami, these two humps of pollution can be seen to grow larger and eventually merge as the day progresses.

If you don't have access to a boat, all you have to do is drive along the elevated portions of Interstate 95 near to downtown Miami during the morning rush hour. Looking east over Biscayne Bay, the sky will normally be relatively free of pollution. But looking west, over the city, one can see a brown pallor hanging low over the city. The smoke coming from the City of Miami's N.W. 12th Avenue incinerator dramatically shows how we are using our sky as a garbage dump.

A final test is the simplest of all: stand near to U.S. 1 during a rush hour and notice the burning sensation in your eyes. This way you can actually *feel* the air pollution problem.

Emission Versus Ambient Pollution Levels
The pollution coming out of a smokestack or from automobile exhaust is usually in a fairly concentrated form. It then disperses and mixes with the pollution from other sources, spreading over a much larger area. If you were to go outside and make an air pollution measurement at some random location not too close to any sources of pollution you would be measuring the *ambient* pollution level—the pollution level for a sample containing pollution from many sources. Such a measurement tells you only how bad the pollution is generally. It tells you very little about where the pollution comes from, who is causing it, or how much is coming from a given source. Thus, you can't really have an effective law to limit ambient pollution levels. You have to limit the *emissions* at the *sources* of pollution. These are the only places where you have much control over pollution. So how do we control the sources of pollution?

Controlling the Sources of Air Pollution
Captain W. T. Guthrie, airline pilot, eloquently expresses the point

of view that air pollution is misplaced private property. It belongs to someone. We have said several times that South Florida has an air pollution problem. Captain Guthrie rightly points out that the *public* does not have an air pollution problem—but some smokestack owner certainly does, for the air pollution that burns my eyes is part of his misplaced property. It comes, for example, from the oil which he burns in his furnace. It is the smokestack *owner's* problem in holding on to his property. It is this owner that should have complete responsibility for managing all of his property, including combustion products.

What are the major sources of air pollution in South Florida? Automobiles (and trucks and buses) are the major polluters of the air of South Florida. In addition, we have the furnaces and smokestacks of several electrical generating stations owned by Florida Power and Light Company, particularly at its Turkey Point facility but also in Dania and in West Palm Beach. There are also several municipal and county incinerators which spew all kinds of nasty rubbish into the sky. This too is misplaced property. It took a recent court order to stop one of the worst offenders, an incinerator called "Old Smokey," owned and operated by the City of Miami in Coconut Grove. During the winter, when old automobile tires are burned in the agricultural areas to prevent frost, portions of South Florida are inundated with a particularly noxious form of air pollution. When the sugarcane fields south of Lake Okeechobee are burned before harvesting, the whole southern portion of the peninsula is frequently blanketed with a thick layer of smoke which resembles the intense smog of Los Angeles.

How do we go about forcing polluters to take better care of their property and hence to stop air pollution at its source? One way would be to pass a law severely restricting emissions of anything other than clean air from any man-made device. This law would have to be backed up by an effective means of enforcement. For example, the fines for a conviction of an air pollution offender would have to be sufficiently high to make it cheaper for the polluter to buy equipment needed to eliminate the pollution than to simply pay the fine and go on polluting.

An alternative way to do the same thing would be to place a tax on the amount of pollution emitted. Again, it would have to be cheaper for the polluter to clean up than to pay the tax and go on polluting.

Unfortunately, however, the practical implications of such a simple solution are not so simple. One of the problems with any air pollution control law lies with the fact that equipment for *measuring* pollution levels (necessary for enforcement of the law) is not able to measure arbitrarily small amounts of pollutants. The enforcement agency may not be able to find (or afford) the equipment required to detect sufficiently small but still dangerous levels of a certain kind of pollution.

Some equipment does exist which is capable of measuring most of the major types of air pollution to extremely small concentrations. Any citizen group looking for an antipollution project to undertake might consider taking a visit to its local pollution control officer to see if he has the equipment he needs to do his job well. If not, that group might start a project to get more money budgeted for the needed pollution detection equipment. The monetary needs of the pollution control officer will probably be found to include also the need for more personnel on his staff—for many of the pollution measurement techniques are time-consuming and elaborate.

But let me warn you of one problem which you may encounter with such a project. To quote *Vanishing Air* by John C. Esposito:

> Some agencies, intoxicated with science, pour most of their manpower and money into monitoring to the neglect of their enforcement responsibilities. . . . The survey and study syndrome has already established itself in many agencies. Federal emphasis on ambient air standards promises to spread the cancer.

As a local example of this, the Dade County Pollution Control Department in 1968 purchased an ambient air quality monitoring device at a cost of $77,000. But, according to Peter P. Baljet, Dade County's new Pollution Control Officer, "The machine has never operated properly. It is presently out of service. In consideration of past difficulties, confidence in the device is totally lacking and it is now up for sale."

Even if it could have been made to work properly this equipment could never have been the least bit effective in either catching a single polluter or in reducing the actual amount of air pollution in Dade County. For, the equipment could measure only *ambient* pollution levels. It would not be able to detect emissions at the sources of pollution.

Before giving the reader the wrong impression, we quote from *Vanishing Air:*

All this is not to say that air monitoring is a waste of time. It can be a useful (if rough) tool for determining *relative* atmospheric changes over a long period. It is essential for future research on the behavior and effects of pollutants and can be employed to discover new problems and potential "hot spots." Moreover, the most sophisticated system will provide some warning, or at least some measure of air pollution episodes. Beyond these limited purposes, though, reliance on [ambient] air quality data—particularly the stuff being churned out today—is thoroughly unwarranted.

Another problem which could be produced by a strict "no emissions" law is that of finding and affording equipment capable of removing all harmful emmissions. No such equipment can remove *all* emmissions completely. One way to overcome this problem might be for the law simply to require polluters to buy and use equipment which is specified by some appropriate agency of the federal or state government to be the best available on the market at the time. The list of acceptable equipment could then be revised every 5 years or so in order to include improvements in the "state of the art" of pollution control.

There are other problems imposed by a strict low-emmissions law. For example, many polluters will tell you that the cost of equipment required to obey the law is so great that it would put them out of business to have to pay for it. While this may be true in certain instances, it certainly doesn't excuse the polluter from having to control his property. We can point out that polluted air also costs. It costs the public physical and mental irritation, sickness, and even shortened lives.

One also hears the statement: "What do you want? Clean air or jobs? You can't have both." It may be true that certain very marginal industries can't operate profitably without polluting the environment. These industries operate with such a small profit margin that *any* increase in costs is apt to put them out of business. They are on shaky grounds to begin with, and the added cost for pollution abatement would be the last straw. These industries probably should not be operating in the first place. A company shouldn't begin business at all if it can't do so without polluting. If a company finds that it has to shut down to obey the air pollution laws, it should do so willingly and its employees should willingly seek employment elsewhere. Federal or state support for these employees while they are looking for other work is highly desirable. Writing and submitting legislation to provide this support would be an excellent project for a young legislator or other concerned group to undertake. In addition it would seem that the growing pollution control industry itself would be an appropriate place for the displaced workers to go. Perhaps we should begin now to replace lost polluting industries with new *anti*-pollution industries such as sewage treatment plants and waste recycling firms.

Given a large industry now finding itself in this predicament, however, how can we make it stop polluting and keep it from going out of business? Being composed of compassionate human beings, the public should, in justifiable cases, find ways of helping the polluter obtain the necessary equipment in a manner that will not put him out of business. It can do this by allowing him to buy the equipment a little at a time, or even by using a little public tax money to help him pay for it. But this should only be done if the company can prove beyond a shadow of a doubt that it will not be making any excessive profit by so doing. If consumers don't like the idea of subsidizing the company with public tax money, perhaps the polluter should be allowed to increase his prices a little to offset the cost of the equipment. But, again, this should be done only if the polluter can prove to the public that the price increase is solely to pay for the anti-pollution equipment (or some portion thereof).

Other Kinds of Air Pollution

I have so far concentrated on combustion products, particularly carbon monoxide, as the major pollutants in South Florida's air. Lest I leave the reader with the false assumption that these are the only pollutants he has to worry about, I shall point out that there are indeed others. For example, there are compounds of the heavy metals, like lead or mercury, which come from many sources, and airborne pesticides, such as DDT. The latter is still used somewhat extensively in the agricultural regions, but can only be used in Florida with a permit from the Florida Department of Agriculture.

There is another, rather innocent looking pollutant which must not be overlooked: asbestos. Its use has grown a thousandfold in the past fifty years. It is often used as insulation for air ducts and is thus carried into the air we breathe by the air conditioning systems of our offices, schools, and churches. To quote again from *Vanishing Air*:

> We know it as a remarkable material which is highly resistant to heat, which does not burn, and which is, in fact, virtually indestructible. It is this very indestructibility, however, which allows asbestos to remain in the lungs for very long periods of time. As the cleansing mechanisms of the lung try to remove this material, "asbestos bodies" are formed. These are often harmless growths but may become cancerous.

And from a study by Litton Industries:

> Asbestos is an air pollutant which carries with it the potential for national or worldwide epidemic of lung cancer or mesothelioma of the pleura or peritoneum. Asbestos bodies have been observed in random autopsies of one-fourth to one-half of the population of Pittsburgh, Miami, and San Francisco and will probably be found in the people of every large city. . . . the effects of the asbestos being inhaled today may not be reflected in the general health of the population until the 1990's or the next century.

Legislative Action

It was said earlier that one way to stop air pollution would be to pass a law severely limiting harmful emissions. But who should pass the law, and who should enforce it?

One usually starts with the local governments. Since in South Florida the problem is not really confined to any single municipality but crosses city limits, one should probably start no lower than the county governments. But the county governments are usually quite accessible to pressure from local industrial polluters. Since most of the pollution comes from private automobiles in South Florida, one should perhaps begin by attempting to get a strong auto emissions control ordinance passed. For many rather obvious reasons, this approach can hardly be successful without a massive attempt at public education. And it certainly will *not* be successful unless an acceptable alternative to the highly polluting automobile engine is available to all car owners in the area. Unfortunately, if the major automobile manufacturers don't provide it, an acceptable alternative will not be available. So it looks as if we are immediately thrust up to the federal level. What hope have we of getting some federal help on this problem? Let us again quote from Esposito's *Vanishing Air.*

In 1967 a piece of legislation which was billed as comprehensive was finally enacted by Congress under the tutelage of Senator Edmund S. Muskie of Maine. The old programs were retained— research, national standards for automobile emissions, federal abatement, technical assistance and grants to the states. But the Air Quality Act of 1967, as it is called, also set up a scheme whereby the federal government would encourage the states to adopt standards for the most polluted regions within their jurisdiction . . . . Suffice it to say at this point, however, that the problem has not been solved. Despite the large, though still inadequate, increase in funding for air pollution activities from a few million dollars in the 1950's to a projected 112 million dollars in 1971, the federal presence and federal leadership have been minimal. . . .

Shortly after the signing of the Air Quality Act of 1967, NAPCA Commissioner John T. Middleton heralded the beginning of "a new era in air pollution control, an era during which the knowledge we now have about how to control pollution will be systematically and scientifically applied across the country." That was 1967. Predictions have a way of coming back to haunt their makers, and the fact is that Commissioner Middleton has not made the most modest beginnings toward a promise to deliver us into a new era of air pollution control. The Task Force found no systematic and scientific application of pollution control knowledge. Instead it found a disorganized band of government officials acting out a pollution control charade. For a few individuals, this game amounts to personal and professional tragedy. For the nation, the game may lead to environmental disaster.

An example of this charade is being acted out right now in South Florida, for the state is in the process of setting and attempting to decide on a way to enforce the unenforceable "ambient air pollution standards" for the NAPCA-designated Southeast Florida Air Quality Control Region.

In a recent newsletter from the Conservation Foundation, it is pointed out that public pressure for more urgent and drastic air pollution control measures has placed the country at the crossroads. But there is a glimmer of hope, says CF:

> Congress is now considering legislation which seeks to lay the groundwork for a major breakthrough in the campaign against air pollution. The carefully worded legislation embodies some drastic new concepts, some severe new restrictions, and some heavy new responsibilities and costs. It challenges basic economic and social canons. It envisions the imposition of blunt restraints on environmentally irresponsible economic growth, land use, and automobile driving. It looks to a day when the air is so clean as to have *no* adverse effects. And it advances the theory that the ordinary citizen has a right to go to court and force industry and government to protect his environment. The proposal thus has a significance broader than air pollution control itself.

The bill in question is H. R. 17255, a complete overhaul of the current Clean Air Act. The House passed its version of the bill on June 10, 1970, and the Senate on September 22. With the advantage of a later and more detailed look at the problem, the Senate proposed a tougher and more far-reaching bill.

The proposed legislation has such great promise, in a time of such great need, that it seems almost too good to be true. We have heard a lot of promises before. But this writer feels the legislation to be so important that he has included mention of it even though the bill may have become severely crippled in the Senate and House conference committee where it was being considered at the time of publication of this book. On December 16, 1970, House-Senate conferees reached final agreement, imposing an absolute legislative deadline of Jan. 1, 1976, for auto-industry production of a virtually pollution-free engine. The implications of this legislation are so great that every American should be intimately aware of its ultimate outcome.

As with any similar piece of public property subject to private exploitation, air will become clean and will remain so only through constant vigilance by the public itself. We will have to be alert, well-informed, and sometimes even a bit nasty if we are to keep polluters in line and the law enforcers doing their job well. The right to breathe clean air is more inherent than the right to pollute it. We are therefore justified in taking a hard line against those who would pollute it.

THE AUTOMOBILE: SERVANT OR MASTER?

Felipe J. Prestamo

Each year an increasing number of Americans decide to have a mechanical servant which promises to provide a basic service to its owner: to take care of his transportation needs. The name of this servant is the automobile.

Americans have many reasons to justify their selection of the automobile as a servant. The prospective automobile owner may think that the entire American society has been organized to put him in the driver's seat, but sooner or later a doubtful thought comes into his mind. It seems too good to be true! As often happens, problems will arise and the efficiency and value of the servant will be questioned. He will probably find that a list of the number of complaints he has about his mechanical servant will be longer than his list of advantages.

Disadvantages

Let us look at the disadvantages for a moment. The promise of unlimited mobility is severely limited by a number of factors. Criss-crossing networks of streets are not able to accommodate peak traffic demands. Driving bumper-to-bumper becomes a sad reality for more and more of the time, and the dependability of the servant comes to be seriously questioned.

If owner and servant are going to the airport, early in the morning or late in the afternoon, they will face the possibility of a traffic jam or even the lack of a convenient parking space. Many would-be air travelers have been forced to reschedule flights because the car was not able to deliver its promise as a reliable means of transportation. This sort of thing has begun to happen so often that the excuse of a traffic

Mr. Prestamo is associate professor of architecture at the University of Miami and is in charge of the courses on environmental planning within his department. He holds the M.S. degree in city planning from the Massachusetts Institute of Technology.

jam or parking problems is probably the most used excuse in the repertory of late-comers.

The auto provides status, but as with many other status symbols, it is a changing one. Continuing changes in models and new trends in style will demand buying a new car every few months in order to possess the latest model.

The list of extra gadgets changes continuously and many Americans have already realized that they are fighting a losing battle in trying to keep up with the automobile industry.

Another inconsistency in our transportation system is the fact that maximum speeds permitted by law in our expressway system are 60 or 70 miles per hour, but the automobile industry keeps offering options of more than 100 miles per hour. The overcrowding of roads makes it impossible to achieve even these high speeds in many cases. The number of fatal accidents in the so-called hot-engine group is rising continuously. Here we have a most outrageous case of an industry inducing its customers to break the law.

Even though the number of cars that you *may* own is unlimited, the *cost* of owning a second or third car takes a heavy toll in many family budgets. The benefits of these additional servants claimed by automobile manufacturers is questionable. In many cases the additional automobile spends eight or nine hours of the day just sitting in a parking lot at work, taking up space. Most of the rest of the time it is parked in the driveway at home. Parking lots and garages are taking huge amounts of land, land that could otherwise be used for other things, such as parks or other recreational facilities. The ridiculous inefficiency of this system, with most automobiles parked for many more hours than they are used, is obvious to anyone who cares to think about it.

Looking at the financial picture, we see that "easy credit" and "easy payment terms" are usually accompanied by high interest rates which further deplete the family finances. Maintenance costs provide the worst part of the entire picture, especially when one considers the time lost by the owner.

We cannot overlook the more general faults of the system, those that affect the entire population, car owners and non-owners alike. The automobile is one of the major polluters of the air. Automobile junkyards are destroying the beauty of the American landscape.

Automobile advertising has created some of the ugliest sights and sounds known to humanity. The assault upon our senses via the automobile advertising media is gigantic and nearly unbelievable, when put in perspective.

Automobile and automobile-related lobbies have influenced the formulation of public policy in a very substantial way. This has had a dramatic effect on our environment and even the thinking of our public officials.

The sad conclusion from all this is that our mechanical servant, the automobile, is not indeed our servant but has become master over us. It is the virtual owner of our metropolitan environment.

The automobile, as a master over us, is not willing to accept restrictions which we may wish to impose on his despotic enterprise. It will require a concentrated effort from the American people in order to properly subdue this arrogant dictator.

The Causes of the Dominance of the Automobile

In order to understand the meaning of automobile dominance within our society, let us take a look at its kingdom, the American metropolis. Urban America has large metropolitan areas acting as nerve centers for a very complex structure. Location of facilities within these metropolitan areas will be dictated by the most efficient combination of accessibility and transportation cost. At this point, the automobile becomes the key factor, as the master of the existing transportation system it dictates the location, size, and even shape of the facilities that are going to serve the American people. Even our residential areas are captives of our intricate network of transportation facilities. One is not free to locate his home in a place where he wants to and which is the the most environmentally sound location, but he must go where the urban market, largely shaped by accessibility criteria, allows him to go!

The shopping activity of the American people is dominated by the automobile. A very small percent of Americans walk to the neighborhood store to buy their weekly food supply. Shopping trips represent a sizeable portion of the traffic which clogs our streets. In Dade County it is estimated that in 1985, twenty percent of the number of trips the average person makes in his automobile will be for shopping purposes.

Note that industrial site selection is usually made on the basis of minimizing transportation costs and maximizing access to markets. The problem of the mobility of the workers in the new facility is very

66

seldom taken into consideration. The location of an office building is even more important, in view of the larger numbers of people involved. But even here accessibility of employees is not a prime consideration in selecting a site.

Alternatives to the Automobile-Dominated Transportation System.

What are the alternatives open to American society to solve the problems of urban transportation? The most radical one would be to eliminate the automobile entirely from the urban scene. As utopian as this may sound to some people, it is just not possible without a large-scale disruption of our entire system of government, business, and finance.

If we cannot eliminate the car entirely, how can we best use it more efficiently and rationally? There are many ways of achieving this goal. One alternative concentrates on two actions: First, to have a transportation mode capable of serving those needs not now fulfilled (or fulfilled very poorly) by the automobile, and secondly, to try and make improvements in the automobile system wherever possible.

The first of these is considered by many people to involve a simple addition to our transportation system. It can be some sophisticated new electronic gadget or a relatively conventional subway. The idea here is to superimpose a new system of transportation onto portions of the present automobile empire. But it really should not be thought of in this way.

What we need, and what we must do, is to change the *structure* of the city in such a way that the new transportation system will be able to compete with the car, and defeat it on its own terms. The new urban structure must be responsive to the public and will probably involve as an integral part some form of modern rapid transit. At the same time, laws and regulations will have to be changed. The tax base of the automobile empire will have to be reviewed and resources will have to be allocated to both systems, not just to the automobile alone.

The American people will have to accept the fact that both systems are for everyone and must be supported by everyone. A few people will have to sacrifice a certain amount of their freedom of movement in order to make the system feasible. It will not actually be that great a loss, since we have already lost a great deal of our freedom of movement due to overcrowding anyway.

It will take time to develop the new system. For years the system will require public resources in order to compete effectively with the car. The transformation of the urban structure (a basic requirement for public transit) will take years to complete. But we will have to keep a close watch to see that it does not get bogged down in the process. The public transit portion of the system will probably have to be heavily subsidized in order to succeed. It should be free to all citizens.

The cost of the mass rapid transit should be paid for by the local government as a service, in the same way that we have a public library or public parks. The users should not have to pay a fare. The actual cost will be less and more and more people will be motivated to use the transit if it is operated in this manner.

The definite advantage of reducing transportation costs will be to induce people to move close to the transit stations helping to build up ridership to the point that the transit system will really improve the level of service of the entire transportation system. The more efficient use of urban land that can be achieved by a rational redistribution of population generated by new patterns of accessibility will tend to increase revenues from local taxes. For example, a recent report by the Stanford Research Institute pointed out the substantial increase in tax revenue to be generated by a new mass transit system in Los Angeles because of valorization of land in areas close to transit stations. This should be a major source of financing for the system. The entire benefits obtained from these sources will cover probably a substantial part of the operation of the public transit. Heavy subsidization is not new to America. The railroads have received a substantial amount of government subsidy, as have the aviation industry and our newest gadget—the supersonic transport.

The second part of the plan consists in imposing a variety of technical standards upon the automobile industry and on automobile owners. The advertising campaign of the automobile industry will have to be regulated in order to destroy the myth surrounding the car, and last, but not least, the drivers will have to have real training in operation and management of the automobile as one element of a system and as personal property.

There can be no doubt that the American society has the technology and the resources for solving the crisis in our metropolitan transportation system. But there still is a question which remains: Do the American people really want to solve the urban transportation problem? To put it another way we might ask: Are we willing to accept the automobile as our master or shall we put it in its rightful place as our servant?

HOW THE AUTOMOBILE MULTIPLIES THE PROBLEMS OF DADE COUNTY

Juanita Greene

James Russell soon will own three cars. "It's embarrassing," he said. "But there's nothing else I can do." He needs a car for himself, a car for his wife, and a car for his teenage daughter, who recently started working part time. "It annoys me that we have reached the stage where this is the only solution to our transportation problem," said Russell.

Three-car families like the Russells are becoming commonplace among all income groups that can somehow squeeze out the payments. Russell was forced to make what may appear to be an extravagant move because he lives in Miami and is up against one of the harsh facts of city life.

Urban man must transport himself over long distances simply to survive. To get from the place where he lives to the place where he makes a living, the Miami worker travels 10, 20, 30, or more miles a day. Here in Dade, in 91 percent of the cases, the worker moves by automobile. Usually he is alone. One man. One car. The domination of the automobile in the local transportation picture is most confounding. The problems it creates are painfully apparent.

The automobile as used today eats up space, uglifies the scene, pollutes the air, picks the pocketbook with a heavy hand, and terrifies and kills at a routine, predictable pace. Yet, say almost all the important people in state and local transportation, the average Miamian, like the average American elsewhere, is not about to give up his automobile, not even for trips to work. "People love cars next to godliness and maybe above that," said Edward Mueller, Secretary of the Florida Department of Transportation.

So convinced are the road folks of man's attachment to his machine

Juanita Greene is urban affairs writer for the *Miami Herald*. This chapter first appeared in the *Miami Herald* on September 13, 1970 and is reprinted here by permission of the Miami Herald Publishing Company.

that they are offering him virtually no other means of moving himself from place to place in the congested city. As a result their declarations are confirmed, their prophesies fulfilled. With no other mode of transportation that would get him to work in about the same length of time at about the same cost, the motorist will indeed stay behind the wheel.

Of the millions to be spent this year on transportation in Dade County by local, state, and federal agencies, all but a drop in the bucket will go for roads. For mass transit—public transit, as they call it today—there is money only for more surveys and some new air conditioned buses to replace the old hot ones on existing routes.

Nothing is in the works to bring to reality such much discussed projects as:

(1) Using the Florida East Coast Railway right of way for some sort of fast public transportation system.

(2) Building a major transportation terminal in downtown Miami.

(3) Running "mini-buses" around downtown Miami and other congested areas.

Perhaps the most significant achievement in public transit the past year was a decision by the state highway planners to include bus boarding ramps and commuter parking lots at intervals along three future expressways. But no financing is yet available for these expressways. In the meantime, what public transit is available gets bogged down in traffic jams, tied up in red tape and parsimonious public policy, or efficiently serves a limited population by operating somewhat outside the law.

Buses we have, the bulk of them operated by the Metro Transit Authority. But they are forced to get out there on the roads and compete for running room with thousands of private vehicles. They get no help and often considerable interference from existing traffic regulations. Not even the simple solution of taking parking off arterial streets to make room for bus lanes seems possible of accomplishment without a revolution.

Further crippling the county bus system is the Metro Commission's decision to force it to pay for itself, out of the fare box. This means buses run mainly where there is money to be made.

Because bus service is so limited, only nine percent of Dade County's work force depends on it for transportation. Adding some pathos to the statistics is the revelation that of the bus-riding workers, an overwhelming majority—eighty-eight percent—are "captives." They own no car and have no other way to get about. Most are poor. Fueling the figures with social significance are the women in their fifties who make up the largest group of MTA customers.

There are taxis in Dade County, but their number is kept limited and their rates kept high by regulation. Most start out at 50 cents, gulp down dimes every three and a half blocks and, when idling, every minute. To go from downtown Miami to Miami International Airport it costs around $5.50 plus tip.

A freeze was put on the issuance of cab certificates three years ago, so today one sells from $12,000 to $15,000. These permits to operate cabs seldom are owned by the drivers, who get only 40 percent of the take by driving for the most affluent owner, who may own dozens of certificates.

One of the many problems plaguing the cab industry is jurisdiction. Cities can issue certificates but if the cab crosses the limits line, the owner has to get another one from the state in order to go into the unincorporated area from each of the other cities he serves. "This cab business in Dade County has been nothing but a headache," said the lady who shuffles the papers for the Florida Public Service Commission.

Also transporting people in Dade County are jitneys. They are mongrel vehicles, a cross between a bus and a taxi. They are allowed only in two Negro areas. By stretching the law they assist many of the poor in getting to work downtown or in Miami Beach for the same fare as the bus but with more speed and camaraderie. Spreading jitney service to other areas so the more affluent could share in the benefits of the poor would meet with powerful opposition from the publicly owned bus company and the privately owned cabs.

Beside lip service, public transit in Dade County is getting $400,000 for a technical study by outside consultants to follow up on a larger transportation study completed last year. The larger study—the Miami Urban Area Transportation Study which projected Dade's total transportation needs for the next 15 years—took five years and cost $1.2 million, most of which was paid by the federal government.

It predicted the need for a rapid transit system and suggested elevated rail cars for some areas and bus expressways for others, but did not get specific about routes and equipment. The current study will tell what kind of rapid transit system should be built, where it should go, and how much it will cost. Two-thirds of the cost of this study is being paid for by the federal government.

To upgrade the existing MTA system, the federal government will give Metro about $4 million to buy 200 new air conditioned buses.

On roads, however, more than $20 million probably will be spent in Dade in the next year. Most of the money will come from the gasoline tax and be channeled through federal, state, and county agencies. Each unit shares in the take from the tax. In addition, three proposed new expressways to be financed by tolls are expected to get at least into the planning stage before next summer.

The local ratio for expenditure on roads versus public transit is similar to the national. The current federal budget provides for an outlay of $4,588 million for highways and only $280 million for urban mass transit.

What money is being spent around the nation for alternatives to auto transportation will come from this mass transit fund. Though small in comparison to the highway budget, it is large enough to provide the main thrust nationwide for mass transit.

Even as they prepare to spend more millions on roads this year, highway officials are beginning to acknowledge that new ones don't always ease traffic jams. From somewhere come enough new autos to clog them up, too. "We can't build roads fast enough to keep up with the need," said Mueller, "because we can't get money fast enough."

Then another problem arises, as explained by State Department of Transportation District Engineer Arnold Ramos, after agreeing that I-95 through Dade County, and especially its giant 36th Street Interchange, is overburdened. "We could relieve this expressway if we built some more," he said. "But people don't want more expressways."

Ramos was referring to resistance of homeowners in north Dade County to the building of additional high-speed roads through their neighborhoods. At public hearings they have appeared en masse to express fear of being forced to move or being sealed off from the remainder of the community.

The status of many of Dade's road projects remains indefinite, even those included in the state's budget. A project that gets in the budget isn't necessarily a project that will be built. Local public officials have learned not to count their roads until construction begins.

Both the county and the state are giving high priority and abundant funds for roads and an interchange that will bring relief to extreme northeast Dade, and other areas. Here the last large tracts of vacant land are being covered over with high-rise residential developments.

Long-range plans call for building many more expressways all over Dade County. In time if plans already laid are completed, a tight gridiron of concrete will cover all the habitable part of Dade County. In between will be room for parking lots and little else.

SOLID WASTE DISPOSAL PROBLEMS
IN SOUTH FLORIDA

Ross McCluney

Most people don't like to think about what happens to their garbage once they have thrown it out. This is understandable, since it is such a messy subject. But many people who know about natural resources and solid waste management tell us that garbage is one of our most significant environmental problems.

To understand why this is so, we note that all the goods we buy in the store come from the earth's natural resources, and nearly all of these goods ultimately end up as garbage and sewage. Waste disposal, as now practiced, is just another name for natural resource depletion. For, with current methods, our raw materials follow a one-way trip from the earth through production and consumption to the garbage dump. There is a problem at both ends of this consumptive highway. Let us look at each separately.

Depletion of Natural Resources.

All the many and varied products which are offered for sale in our expanding economy have their origin in the earth—its natural resources. The amount of these resources is limited. There is only so much earth for us to consume. And yet, the number of people on earth continues to skyrocket upward and the amount of goods (and hence resources) which each one consumes is also rising rapidly. Thus, depletion of our natural resources is becoming a very real threat.

In a recent book, *Moment in the Sun*, Robert and Leona Rienow note that official charts and reports are available which clearly show the depletion of our raw materials. And yet, the "wizards of industry" stoutly assert that "nowhere in the foreseeable future" can they detect any scarcity which would hobble our genius in gadgetry or force us to deny ourselves all the fancy gadgets which the wizards of expansionism are so anxious to give us.

The Rienows explain the discrepancy between these two views by first pointing out that the huge stockpiles of seemingly limitless iron ore are of very low grade; the high grade ore is already gone. In addition, population increases and greater demands will place strong pressures on forests, which produce the raw material used to manufacture paper and other wood fiber products. The National Forest Service estimates that by 1985 the demand for wood and wood fiber will exceed the annual growth in our forests. Similar situations exist with our supposedly limitless supply of other resources as well.

Thus we have become the victims of a statistical hoax fostered on us by the giants of industry with their idolatrous devotion to an ever-expanding economy as the god of success and prosperity. To quote the Rienows:

> The second trick of the wizards of promotion is not illusion but legerdemain. It consists of attracting so much attention to the GNP, the finished product of our industrial genius, that we neglect to observe where more and more of the *raw resources* are coming from to maintain this American superiority in production. We are so mesmerized by the limitless flow of finished goods that we do not think to question our ever increasing dependence on other nations for raw materials or what this trend may some day mean to us.
>
> Natural resources impoverishment, of course, when it reaches a certain critical point, signals our permanent eclipse as the world's first power. We are used to thinking of ourselves as a "surplus nation," and up until 1940 this was roughly so. We produced more raw materials than we consumed. . . .
>
> By 1952 thirty-three separate minerals had entered the "critical" list. "Nor can the United States indefinitely depend on the rest of the world for its mineral needs at the present rate of consumption."
>
> "With only 6 per cent of the world's population, the United States has in the past used enough ore to account for half the world's steel output, and has consumed more than half the world's oil and about nine-tenths of its natural gas." . . .

Only a few resources are still sufficient for domestic demands. We can now, however, proceed to exhaust other nations' as we have our own.

The Rienows list many more such natural resources for which the nation will increasingly turn outside its borders. Here, then, is a nation, the envy of the world, that is consuming the world's reserves of minerals and fuels at an almost terrifying rate.

Clearly, some way must be found to reduce the impact our hyper-consumptive economy is having on the natural resources of the world. And yet we dash on blindly, pursuing the wrong goals, the wrong priorities. The wizards of industry still cry, for example, that if the United States does not proceed to develop its own supersonic transport it will lose its position of dominance in air travel. If they were really concerned about the position of the United States in world markets, they would be crying for a crash program to stop the drain on our nonrenewable resources. For we have already lost our position of dominance in this vital area.

Reducing the Drain on Our Natural Resources

In searching for a solution to this problem, we can think of two possibilities which can be undertaken simultaneously. One is to reduce the amount of resource depletion itself, by producing less and consuming less. In particular, we should eliminate unnecessary waste such as excess packaging and "disposable" products. The other is to recycle the valuables which we do throw away. We must go out to the garbage dump and salvage as many of the discarded resources as we can, in order to return them as raw materials to the beginning of the production cycle. That is, we must begin a massive recycling program immediately.

We haven't yet begun to feel very strongly the effects of natural resource depletion. There are still those that say we are not in danger. The threat does not appear to be immediate. Americans (and people in general) have an annoying way of ignoring imminent large-scale disaster until it gets very close. So perhaps we should look for a more immediate threat. Let's examine present methods of waste disposal for a more direct reason to justify our obvious need for massive recycling. Let us look, in particular, at some of the waste disposal problems of Dade County.

Solid Waste Management in Dade County

In Dade County, approximately 40 to 60 percent of the people (those in the unincorporated areas of the county) are served by the Dade County Waste Division. The remaining are served by municipal and private haulers. To simplify our considerations let us look at what happens to the waste collected by just the Metropolitan Dade County Waste Division. Presently, all of the waste collected by the Waste Division is placed in sanitary landfills. In this operation, cells or pits are dug to bedrock or ground water. The depth of these cells is usually about 3 feet, but may be greater. They are usually about 200 feet by 350 feet in area. The waste is layered in and covered each day with six inches of earth, except in periods of peak loads when manpower and equipment are all involved in dumping, with little time left for covering. Each pit is built up to no more than 8 feet above the original ground level and then is covered with a final layer of earth two feet thick.

The county is presently using three landfills, with a total area of 1,040 acres, of which about 34 percent remains to be filled. Mr. W. B. Byrd, assistant superintendent of the Waste Division, and Mr. Carl Aaron, pit foreman, estimate that the remaining land should last another 10 years. When it does run out, the county will have to either seek additional land or start reusing old landfills.

It should be noted that after several years of decomposition and proper preparation, the land on top of a sanitary landfill can be developed into a public park or a residential subdivision. Thus it is conceivable that the county could, in ten years, simply trade its filled land for another, unfilled site.

It is also possible, however, that as the population continues to grow and as available land becomes more and more developed, Dade County might find itself in the same situation as New York City, which has run out of places to put its waste and is in a rather difficult position.

In order to eliminate this possibility (at least temporarily), Dade County is relying on another way out. This is incineration. By burning waste in a high temperature furnace, the volume occupied by the waste can be reduced by as much as 85 percent, thus buying time without having to reuse old landfills or purchase new land. However, the burning of municipal wastes in incinerators can produce some of the filthiest air pollution around. The big question is whether the county will be willing to put out the necessarily high expenditures in order to insure that the new incinerators will be "clean." It is not really certain whether an adequately clean method of incineration can be found at all.

Dade's Waste Division should soon find out. Its new northeast incinerator (the only one operated by the county) is in operation for tests and should be in full operation shortly, handling up to 300 tons of waste per day. So far, air pollution measurements made by a private consulting firm show that the facility is capable of meeting the Metro air pollution ordinance. The firm of consulting engineers which is making the tests is even putting up a bond to guarantee it.

The only kind of pollution control equipment being used in this incinerator is a device called an electrostatic precipitator which removes particulates from the stack effluent. It does not remove any of a variety of poisonous gases which can be produced by combustion in the furnace. According to Al Rebus, Acting Chief Engineer with the Dade County Pollution Control Department, particulates are the only pollutants you have to worry about with this incinerator. To make sure, his group of engineers will perform a test called an Orsat analysis, to measure levels of carbon monoxide, carbon dioxide, and nitrogen, before the plant is opened for full operation. Unfortunately, this test will not measure a variety of other gases which can be generated by combustion of household wastes. Some of these gases are highly poisonous, such as those produced when certain kinds of plastic are burned.

In spite of this, Dade County is moving ahead with its plans to put the incinerator into full operation. It will not find the Pollution Control Department standing in its way, since it doesn't appear that the incinerator will be in violation of the pollution control ordinance. If this plant proves to operate successfully (at full capacity and without violating the law), other incinerators are sure to follow, with the county planning to eventually incorporate all existing incinerators (including municipally owned incinerators such as the City of Miami's "Old Smoky" incinerator) into a network of eight incinerators to handle all solid wastes in the county. So in a few years we are sure to have one or two more county incinerators in operation, puffing away without visible smoke, but perhaps likely to be containing a variety of invisible but deadly gases, all perfectly legally.

But what if the county or the state comes along and passes a stricter air pollution control law? Both Peter Baljet and Dennis Carter (assistant to the County Manager) agree that the county will have to comply. Mr. Carter points out, however, that you can't pass a law that is impossible to meet. Air pollution laws are not likely to be passed which require better pollution control equipment than industry can produce. The unfortunate thing about this is that it can produce a state of affairs in which dangerously high pollution levels are permitted legally simply because we don't have the equipment available which can burn garbage and do so without polluting. This author doubts very seriously whether incineration will be an effective *long range* answer to our mounting waste disposal problems.

In such a case wouldn't it be better to just stop burning garbage altogether? We find ourselves victims of what Gene Marine calls "the engineering mentality." People who operate with this point of view believe that if one engineering fix (the incinerator) doesn't work, you try another (the electrostatic precipitator). If this one doesn't work (because of a future passage of a tougher antipollution law) then you try still another (more expensive equipment aimed at further fixing up a technique that was faulty from the beginning).

Such people are guilty of having "tunnel vision." They can only see in one direction, that of a long series of engineering fixes, each one designed to compensate for the deficiencies of the previous one. They are somehow unable to ask the question: "Did we really need the first engineering fix in the first place?" They can't even conceive of the possibility that perhaps a completely different approach should have been taken all along.

What is needed is a large-scale recycling system for solid wastes as an appropriate alternative to incinerators with expensive air pollution control devices attached.

To give another example of the use of the engineering fix to fix the engineering fix, remember the Coconut Grove incinerator of the City of Miami. When "Old Smokey" was built in 1961 at a cost of $1.5 million it immediately invoked protests because of soot deposits from its belching stack. After 9 years and $100,000 worth of "improvements," Old Smokey still had to be closed down for excessive air pollution. The City of Miami now plans to spend some $2.4 million to double Old Smokey's capacity and to install pollution control devices. One technological fix produces another. We can only wait and see how effective Old Smokey's latest "improvements" will be.

So far we have indicated that the present method of landfill may be satisfactory for a few more years. But there is some doubt about this.

On a national scale, the U.S. Department of Health, Education, and Welfare states that "ninety-four percent of all land disposal operations and 75 percent of municipal incinerators are unsatisfactory from a standpoint of public health, efficiency of operation, or protection of natural resources." Locally, Peter Baljet, the Dade County Pollution Control Officer says: "With the relatively high ground water in Dade County there appears to be a danger of harmful substances from these so-called sanitary landfills penetrating into our water supply. We have no factual data to substantiate this effect but we are aware of a proposed study sponsored by the Dade County Health Department in conjunction with the U.S. Geological Survey to determine the influence of present sanitary landfill operations in Dade County on our underground water supply. I think that this study will show a definite flow of harmful materials such as compounds of the heavy metals and other toxic substances into the aquifer."

At any rate, even though the county's future plans for waste disposal remain in doubt, it appears that we may be able to get by for a few more years with the present method of waste disposal.

But do we really have this much time? What if the county is forced to abandon its plans for incineration because it cannot meet new federal or state air pollution requirements? What if it can't find suitable land to continue its landfill operations in the eight to ten years left? What if present landfill operations are shown to be hazardous to public health? We had better start now to look realistically at the alternatives and use our remaining few years to plan for the future.

This is where the natural resource depletion part of the picture comes in. We are looking for a method of waste disposal that:

(1) Doesn't need new land.
(2) Doesn't pollute the air or the ground water.
(3) Is cheaper than the present method.
(4) Doesn't deplete natural resources.

The generally accepted solution to these four requirements is recycling. Recycling is actually just another name for economizing. To recycle is to reuse our discarded raw materials. A considerable technology is now being built up around this concept.

Techniques of Recycling

Most of the waste recycling systems which have been proposed involve the use of a mechanical separator which attempts to sort

80

garbage (or incinerator residues) into separate piles of glass, aluminum, paper, plastic, wood, and food wastes, for example. Separation is technically difficult to achieve. Available equipment is only partially successful. But once the garbage *has* been properly separated, the remainder of the recycling method is quite easy and straightforward to accomplish.

Glass waste is sold to companies which either melt it down for reuse or crush it for use in such things as glass wool insulation and building bricks, or as a substitute for crushed limestone aggregate in asphalt for paving streets. To quote Richard L. Cheney, Executive Director of the Glass Container Manufacturers Institute: "At the present time, we in the glass container industry see salvage and reuse as the only long-range solution to the waste problem. The conservation of raw materials demands salvage, and the long-range, efficient management of waste calls for reuse. We are convinced that salvage will materially reduce pollution."

Aluminum wastes are sold to aluminum manufacturing companies which are eager to get them. Much less electrical energy (and hence pollution) is needed to resmelt the refined aluminum of soft drink and beer cans than to extract aluminum from the ore. Paul Murphy, vice-president of the packaging division of Reynolds Metals, stated in November 1969 that "the potential reclamation value of these cans is enormous . . . . Even as small a return as ten percent would bring in a substantial amount of money." Reynolds now offers a half-cent bounty for every all-aluminum can turned in at a pilot station in Los Angeles. It has recently extended this program to New York City and Miami. The *Miami Herald*'s "Action Line" column recently stated:

> The metals reclamation department of Reynolds Aluminum has been very busy in the Miami area for the past three years. They have installed Goodwill boxes in 167 shopping centers in the Miami area for the collection of all-aluminum cans. Goodwill Industries picks the cans up from the boxes and receives 10 cents a pound from Reynolds. Immediately after Jan. 1, 1971 Reynolds will set up a collection center at 4450 Ponce de Leon Blvd. where aluminum cans will be bought at a half-cent each.

Paper wastes are sold to paper companies for direct reuse. Approximately 20 percent of the fiber used in paper products is recycled paper, according to the Forest Products Laboratory of the

U.S. Forest Service. Some fiber-poor nations recycle more. About half of the wood fiber volume consumed in Japan and West Germany consists of reclaimed fiber. There are some mills in the United States dealing with 100 percent reclaimed fiber and making fairly high grade products. We need more of these. The depletion of our forest resources will be critical by the end of this decade. Recycling can help buy us more time. Ultimately we shall have to control population as well.

Food wastes can be turned into valuable fertilizer by composting. There is a growing demand for suitable compost material among organic and other types of farmers. Organic farmers believe (and demonstrate) that high quality and quantity foods can be grown without use of pesticides and most other chemicals.

Thus, we see that the technology *and the demand* for most waste materials exists now and is ready for further expansion. The only real holdup seems to be the problem of sorting municipal wastes into the categories listed above.

Two approaches are presently undergoing experimentation. One attempts to sort the residues left after incineration and the other attempts to sort the garbage itself, before incineration. Since incineration destroys many of the valuable components of garbage and tends to produce air pollution, the latter operation is the more desirable of the two. By sorting the garbage itself, one can, at least theoretically, retain most of the recycling value that is present when the waste is picked up. Unfortunately, however, this method has not been quite as successful as one would like.

A third method can be proposed. With this method the various types of waste products are kept separate from the start, thereby eliminating the need for the sorting step. This is obviously the most efficient and economically valuable method of all except for one thing. Everyone considering this method assumes that it will fail due to lack of cooperation from the public. It is assumed that people will not be willing to take the extra effort to keep their glass, metal, paper, and food wastes separate all the way from the grocery store to the garbage can. As a result there is a strong reluctance to design systems and devices to help them in such an effort, so the task seems to be doomed to failure from the start. It is the writer's opinion, however, that given sufficient financial and other incentives, together with the necessary technological support, the public can indeed be encouraged to accept this most efficient means of recycling.

As an example of the technological support which would be needed, architects and builders would have to begin including appropriate waste disposal systems in the houses that they produce. The design might include such things as a kitchen counter top with five large holes at the back which lead by way of chutes to a five-compartment garbage can. Garbage trucks would then have to be designed with five separate compartments in order to keep the trash components separate the rest of the way to the central recycling depot. The incentive to operate such a system could come from giving the garbage collectors a share in the proceeds from the recycling depot and therefore also providing an improvement in the status of the garbage collector in our society. The homeowner could be encouraged to participate by being paid for his garbage rather than being charged a collection fee.

Although the author cannot demonstrate the overall economic feasibility of the proposed system, he feels that the plan has sufficient merit to warrant its evaluation among the other proposals. Dade County, and perhaps some of the municipalities facing similar problems, should begin pilot projects at once in order to investigate ways of implementing recycling on a community-wide scale. Feasible beginnings might be found in multi-unit buildings such as apartments and condominiums.

As our population grows and our needs continue to multiply, how much longer can we afford to throw away in municipal refuse a billion dollars worth of iron, aluminum, copper, lead, zinc, and tin every year? Now that gold and silver have become important industrial metals, can we continue to afford the annual waste of millions of ounces of these precious metals in the careless discard of such items as photographic film, costume jewelry, solder, outmoded computer circuits, and similar products? As our requirements for living space and recreational areas keep mounting, can we remain tolerant of the practices that clutter valuable land surfaces with ugly refuse piles and destroy the natural beauty of a continent?

Questions like these are being asked today in many parts of our country. Almost overnight, it seems, our waste-disposal practices have become a subject of national concern. Our sudden awareness of the problems they pose has coincided with the convergence of national trends in population growth and industrial productivity and with a change in cultural attitudes.

Public money spent nationwide for the collection, treatment, and disposal of wastes is so great that its cost is exceeded only by education and roadbuilding. But in spite of the money we spend, the job is being done poorly. We're making a dump of our entire nation while we could be reclaiming these wastes, saving ourselves millions, and actually beautifying, instead of polluting, the land. Sooner or later we'll *have* to do it—why not start now?

A NEW CONCEPT OF THE VALUE OF LAND

Judith and Ross McCluney

Florida has been sold for decades as an inexhaustible land of sun, water, wildlife, and lush tropical foliage. "A subtropical paradise" was the theme song of the real estate developers in describing their land for homesites to potential residents. Surely they would never have depicted these tracts as drained, filled, leveled off, paved-over burdens on the natural resources of the area. Nor would the new homeowner have dreamed that in purchasing this land he had helped to undermine the area's natural water conservation systems, to degrade coastal estuaries, to destroy the native foliage and wildlife, and to promote urban sprawl with buildings little related to the tropical environment. Yet these have been the frequent results of his actions.

South Floridians daily witness the rapid encroachment of roads, congestion, and residential developments on the natural systems of the area. Even the architecture of most homes and apartments walls off the residents from much exposure to the natural environment. At the present rate of growth and with current approaches to development, it seems to be only a matter of a short time before the dream of South Florida is irreversibly destroyed. So long as our present incomplete concepts of the use and the value of land remain, the ecosystem of South Florida will be locked in a fatal battle with the developer.

The problem was well stated by Aldo Leopold in 1948 in the preface to his book *A Sand County Almanac*:

> Conservation is getting nowhere because it is incompatible with our Abrahamic concept of land. We abuse land because we regard it as a commodity belonging to us. When we see land as a

Mrs. McCluney is a sociologist working for the State of Florida Division of Vocational Rehabilitation. Mr. McCluney is a graduate student in the Department of Physics of the University of Miami.

community to which we belong, we may begin to use it with love and respect. There is no other way for land to survive the impact of mechanized man, nor for us to reap from it the esthetic harvest it is capable, under science, of contributing to culture.

The question arises as to whether there is another system of values on which the use of land can be based. Can we state a new concept of land use which is compatible with conserving and enhancing the environment?

The first tenet of such a concept of land use would be the centering of human life around an overriding respect for nature and the inviolability of the land. Man would recognize his place as an intimate and dependent part of nature, and he would strive not to upset the balance of natural forces. He would strive to live within the carrying capacity of the air, water, and land.

The great American architect Frank Lloyd Wright developed a "new" approach to land use and architectural design. He called it "organic" or natural architecture. He conceived it as an architecture which would arise from the basic relationship of the natural character-istics of the ground with the human spirit and character of the inhabitants. Wright found expressions of "organic" architecture in the buildings of some ancient civilizations—of the early Pacific Islanders, of Japan, of Persia, of Byzantium, of the Mayans. He saw their architecture as being truly creative in those early days in that they were true to the earth.

With the coming of modern technology, however, man became largely cut off from the inspiration of nature and the earth. Wright felt that this came about because, in using increasingly complex machinery, man found an easy way of building in which it was not necessary to become personally involved with the task. In the course of this rush to "civilization," man lost much of his earlier reverence for nature and separated himself from the natural world. Land use and architecture became measured by their money values. They became standardized and uncreative. Thus the basis was established for commercial exploita-tion of what the American Indians considered sacred and inviolate—the American earth.

The American Indian preserved the land. As one example, Dorothy Lee points out in her book *Freedom and Culture* that Dakota Indian children were brought up to feel that they were part of nature and relatives of all things natural—animals, earth, air, and even rocks. She says responsibility toward the buffalo, reluctance to kill wantonly, to waste any of the products of nature, stemmed from this feeling of relatedness to nature. The Indian made careful use of nature's resources and he did not overburden the land. When he moved away, he left the land much as he had found it.

Modern land use can likewise be based on a thorough respect for land. Ian McHarg has developed a set of guidelines, set forth in his book *Design With Nature* and in his other publications and public presentations. He advocates the study of a whole region by a group of experts in many disciplines to determine to what use each piece of land in the region can best be put without causing destruction of the natural assets of that land and of the surrounding community.

McHarg delineates natural rules governing the proper use for various types of land which should be followed in making land-use decisions. For example, beaches in general are built up and maintained by nature typically through a dynamic sand transport system and by such natural bulwarks as vegetation and dunes. There is a certain distance from the beach at which construction of buildings will in no way threaten the preservation of the beach. When man insists on placing buildings closer to the shore than this distance, however, the result is most often damage to or destruction of the beach, the seacoast, the buildings. We have numerous tragic examples of this in South Florida.

Modern civilization has brought man the potential to do tremendous and irreparable environmental damage. The face of the land can be changed with incredible rapidity by our bulldozers and heavy machinery. Once changed, the old balance of nature cannot be restored. It is impossible to replace a mature forest growth or a fertile marsh once destroyed. It is as difficult today to think of a natural stand of trees growing on most of Miami Beach as it is to find the proverbial tree in Brooklyn. In fact, in many areas it is difficult to tell Miami Beach and Brooklyn apart, at least with respect to the amount of concrete and lack of native greenery. Even North Kendall Drive in South Dade, recently semi-rural, no longer has the many tall pine trees characteristic of the area.

To many land developers and other persons, land has value only in terms of the *use* to which it is put by man. All land owned by them *must* be used for some purpose (usually profit-making). One even hears the land developer claim it to be his *right* to profit by the sale or use of land. Wilderness and farm land is often seen by these people to be a wasteland, basically unproductive, valued only in terms of its "potential for development." Some readers may feel that the authors are overemphasizing a stereotyped image of the land developer. While this may be true in some cases, in most it is not, and we feel that such an approach can be quite useful in identifying clearly objectionable values used by these people.

The effect of this often autocratic disregard and misunderstanding of the functions and the relationship of a piece of land to the health of the whole community, to the forces of nature, frequently has been disaster. We see it in the blight of downtown Miami. We see it in the monotonous ugliness of many local housing developments which very likely will someday resemble the decay of Miami slums—aging houses, crowded streets, and few parks or areas of natural beauty to relieve the barrenness and the congestion. Many of these monuments to development are actually instant ghettos. There are other examples of what can happen when one lacks a proper respect for the forces of nature or the welfare of the community.

On Miami Beach, several hotel builders, not understanding the dynamics of wave and wind action and other natural processes, built hotels too close to the beach. Now they wonder what happened when all their beach has washed away. Another group of developers, not understanding the importance of mangroves and other shoreline vegetation and the impact of sewage effluent, built miles of cement walls along the shores of north Biscayne Bay and dumped sewage into it. Now they wonder why the clear water has turned dark and cloudy and has lost many of its fish. Early developers of South Florida, not understanding the role of high water levels inland in pushing back the sea and in keeping our ground water salt-free, drained the land and built on it. Then they wondered what happened when salt water intruded inland and spoiled several freshwater wells near the coast.

These are nature's warnings. Nature has its own set of inviolable rules and regulations. Some of them are known to us and others are not. The penalty for disregarding these rules can be incredibly severe. Nature and man are not two equal partners negotiating over some mutually beneficial arrangement. Nature includes and is ultimately more powerful than man. If you destroy man, nature will be somewhat diminished. If you disregard man's impact on nature, there may be no man.

Not all the rules, and not all the consequences of man's actions, can be foreseen. For this reason, man must be very careful, very yielding, giving nature the benefit of any doubt. If there is any possibility that significant environmental damage might result from a contemplated action, the only possible course is no action at all. If the demands of nature are too great for man to both develop the land and to satisfy his need to live comfortably, he must be prepared to abandon development and leave the land undisturbed.

The environment of South Florida is extremely sensitive to small alterations. It is all low-lying flatland, a natural, shallow flood plain, unified by the dynamics of water flow. It is already threatened by the extremely rapid encroachment of population on its wildlife, vegetation, open space, and its ability to safely assimilate human waste materials.

What future will South Floridians have? If South Florida is to have a livable future, it would seem that we must adopt concepts of land value different from those of past unbridled development. We must place at the foundation of these values a respect for the natural characteristics of our area and our determination to live in harmony with them. We must seek agreement on the features we value and need in our community, and enforce zoning and land use controls to preserve them. We must place limits on population pressures so that we will cease to threaten our water, space, and other natural resources. In all this, we must approach our planning with great care and preparation. If we are successful in establishing our new concept of land values, the end result must be the preservation of the natural integrity of South Florida.

The ability to live within certain environmental guidelines and limits may require some sacrifice from the individual. For example, the landowner may no longer be able to have sole power over the decision as to how to develop his land. The citizen may need to endure, and pay for, stricter controls over disposal of human wastes. The businessman may have to adjust to fewer people crowded into an area and a non-expanding market for his goods. The individual will have to alter some of his expectations and demands in order to gain a healthy community environment. He must also realize that only planning and foresight on the part of his whole community can protect his enjoyment of the natural benefits of his surroundings. Too many unhappy Floridians have understood this only after awakening one day to find their once sunny yards engulfed by the shadow of a new high-rise apartment, or the open field around them replaced by a shopping center. Too many people have purchased lovely homes in the uncrowded suburbs only to find themselves too tired to enjoy them after fighting the traffic-jammed roads.

Another difficulty in trying to live in harmony with nature in South Florida is the lack of architectural styles based on a tropical environment. Some older Florida houses were designed for openness and to take advantage of the prevailing breezes, but newer buildings are rarely built with these in mind. And as a result, the only way to live in them comfortably is to provide them with air conditioners which gulp electricity and increase power-generator-produced pollution of the environment. Likewise, the homeowner who desires to have natural foliage left on his property will have a hard time finding a compliant bulldozer operator when the house is built.

In seeking a house of his own, Miami architect Yiannis Antoniadis became disgusted when realtors could offer him nothing but concrete block rectangles. His goal was to build a house that would create a harmony between himself and nature. He finally designed and built his own home. It is an extremely open plywood module house, suspended above the ground from four telephone poles and placed beneath an old banyan tree which he felt was the most valuable thing on his property. Through this design, Antoniadis eliminated ground dampness, caught the breeze, and received the benefits of the tremendous cooling abilities of the tree.

Often, house designs that build on the gifts of nature can enhance the comfort and the beauty of living without straining natural resources as much as traditional housing does. Cooling by careful orientation of the house to prevailing winds and the use of solar heating are two adaptable ideas. In her book *Environment and Design in Housing,* Lois Davidson Gottlieb states the problem:

Unfortunately, too many of our present-day buildings are based on custom rather than actual need. It is easy to give up thinking about the real needs and assume that traditional ways are "the way" to do things. For example, when man migrated to colder climates thousands of years ago, he developed form-fitting clothes designed particularly for cold climates. Today, even in the most tropical climates, a building is not considered truly modern without a totally artificial atmosphere inside. Then, to achieve maximum efficiency, the windows don't open even if you would like to let in a breath of fresh air.

There is nothing wrong with form-fitting clothes or air-conditioning, but it is worth considering what these things were designed for, and whether it might not be just as pleasant to feel a gentle breeze or hear a passing bird from the window once in a while.

The issue at stake in our choice of values for the land is ultimately human survival. The power of man to destroy the web of life of which he is a part has never before been so great and so extensive. The death of every sparrow and the discarding of every beer can has global environmental significance. The globe has become small, and the land we once thought was never-ending is vanishing into concrete.

AN ARCHITECT LOOKS AT MIAMI

Lester C. Pancoast

From an airplane, or from the top of our tallest buildings, in the morning light, one can see that ours is a magnificent coastal city rising from a dense carpet of green. From a distance, clean and inviting, a stirring vision of promise and opportunity.

Now, descend, look objectively, and react. Is it thin and dreary? Are the buildings mostly tired and colorless? Have most of the streets no trees? Is most of the land paved with cars? Does it seem to spread endlessly? Does it suggest a special way of life in a special climate?

Do its citizens agree on where they are going, or are they environmental fatalists, denying any real responsibility? Who formed this young city of Miami, and how should it be judged? The needs of our uneven growth were balanced against finance, land, management, technology, and labor. These are always the determinants of architecture and planning, with the resulting quality of environment and life style the only indicators of achievement.

An increasing number of us are becoming deeply concerned with the achievement of the urban America we inhabit. Talk with travelers, not necessarily designers, artists, or planners, who have recently returned from places like Europe, Scandinavia, Japan, or Mexico. They often express a sad realization on returning to the home which they love and of which they are proud, that the places they have been were more human and more loved. Why should this be so?

Are we too fast or too selfish or too fractured in the way we build? We have no ancient patterns of life to defend against the automobile. Most of our buildings and their creators do not understand us, and the buildings have nothing to say to each other, as they do in so many

Mr. Pancoast, architect, senior partner of Ferendino/Grafton/Pancoast, is a native Miamian who has recently been involved with various architectural projects in housing, planning, and environmental design. This article is reprinted from *Miami Interaction,* November 1970.

foreign places. Isolated lumps do not make an urban fabric. Our cities are wasteful and chaotic, awash in unqualified and wasted space. We have achieved a forty-mile per hour placelessness, and it is spreading to the places which remain. Architect Benjamin Thompson, who believes that environment is a learning experience "second only to family relationships" calls the American scene "the vast middle-class slum created by business and bureaucratic indifference, sustained by public insensitivity." And he connects that slum to the violence of our social revolution. Which came first, the environment or our culture: Each creates the other.

If conditions are all that bad, what should we do? Senator Gurney has assured us along with Governor Muskie that there are no ways to control South Florida's population. He and most of our prominent citizens want greatness through greater growth. How do we in Dade County avoid much more of the same? Is Kendall Drive the way of our future? We could certainly hope not.

Our far flung sub-urban growth threatens our remaining wilderness. We could merge with Tampa as we have with Palm Beach, and the Everglades would become a drainable inconvenience. As we are poised to strip develop Alligator Alley and Tamiami Trail, our central city cries for rejuvenation and rebuilding.

There is every long-range economic reason to lift our central cities out of their malaise. Because the fabric is so thin in a daytime, almost-city like Miami, it is more easily rebuildable. Now that expressways have connected our core to our outer reaches, there should exist desire as well as need to use the core, and eventually even to live there. This city above all others should invite close examination as a colorful place of tropical urbanism, instead of dealing in anticlimax as a temperate zone city accidentally built in the subtropics.

Most of us in South Florida realize that we are on a frontier of militant (nonviolent) conservationism. For years conservation in this country meant preservation of wild animals and their wild environments. Today, it means primarily the preservation of the animal man, and hopefully also an understanding of the environment he requires to survive, both physically and mentally. Ecology includes us, and Nature is our own house.

Take a simple, often repeated thought from our current newspapers: there can be no more septic tanks built in South Florida without fouling our water supply. Are we really twenty-five years late in beginning to realize that new populations *must* be related to carefully devised, economic utility systems. Here, if we grasp its importance and face the problem, is an urgent check on our sprawl.

In embattled Dade County, conservationists and architects are finding common causes in issues such as the recent Saga Development proposals, which came close to setting a most inhuman environmental standard for the remaining mainland bayfront. The coalition provided the backing needed by the County Commission to affect the Saga plan. And a new pattern has been set for facing approaching major environmental issues on a multi-discipline, professional basis.

If the 1940s, 1950s, and 1960s outspread is recognized by us as undesirable and even dangerous, is it conceivably possible for our government, so superbly responsive to the capabilities and limitations of electorates, to evolve a taxation policy for land and buildings which will lead development in more intelligent directions? Zoning processes, associated with endless rules for conformity and minimum behavior, are beginning in some areas of our country, including Dade County, to offer well devised incentives for enlightened, more imaginative architectural behavior and land use. Taxation, also, gradually adjusted to a guidance policy, could become a needed creative tool if released from merely following property values.

As the expressways have been, mass transit will eventually be superimposed on or above the monotonous automobile street grid. When we have become able to subsidize the necessary hardware and real estate, mass transit will then become another determinant of a reurbanization of Dade County. If one can simultaneously resolve the solutions of the three systems mentioned above, sewers, taxes, and mass transit, he has aptitude for what today is called the "systems approach" to design. Don't let professional technicians frighten you; systems approach is merely balanced selection and design of the interrelated, and is no more difficult than three dimensional chess. But, if we choose to control our growth and create a valid population concentration, our systems must be dealt with first. The Miami area could become one of the world's great urbanizations, but not, we have proven, lump by lump and block by block, endlessly into the wilderness.

It is alarming to realize that we as occupants of a young city, after a period of rapid initial growth, must already question our chances of environmental limitations or even survival, as if we were ancient Mayas facing the problems of Chichen Itza. Most of us feel a sense of helplessness with respect to changing our surroundings. Some of us, however, have greater impact than we imagine, owning buildings, advertising, serving in government. There are important moments of decision for each of us, and "insignificant moves toward significant change." Here is the beginning of a list:

(1) Actively support the organizations which are fighting the environment battles.

(2) Express environmental and urban concerns to politicians.

(3) Build enlightened, sensitive buildings; select qualified local professional help.

(4) Help reduce undesired population increase.

(5) If you need status symbols, place quality above size.

(6) Create enclosures, places without automobiles.

(7) Support neighborhood trees; if there are none, provide them, with intelligent advice.

(8) Make better signs, discover the profitable, enjoyable art of graphics with a graphic designer.

(9) Become a critic; ask questions. Develop and share an opinion.

(10) Eschew the ersatz.

Perhaps it is equally important to make a list of what we can do to pull our fractious population together.

ENVIRONMENTAL DECISION–MAKING

Virginia Hine

There is a common assumption in our society that our leaders make decisions in a logical way and based upon known facts. This assumption is misleading and may be dangerous. We cannot count on our decision-making leaders to actually use ecological facts presented to them by scientists when these leaders make their ecological decisions. I would like to suggest five things which can be just as influential in environment decision-making as known ecological facts.

Environmental Perception.

Environmental perception is the way an individual looks at and thinks about any section of our natural surroundings. As part of our research into the growing conservation-ecology movement, we questioned people who live near the Cocoplum-Tahiti Beach area of Miami. This is a large tract of land on Biscayne Bay in Coral Gables. It has lots of pine trees, a few dirt roads, some canals, and lots of weeds and bushes. We asked each householder to describe the Cocoplum area and then to say what he would do with it if the decision were his to make. We found out that people who used negative words to describe the area (such as "wasteland," "buggy," "useless," etc.) favored the fullest urbanization of it (big apartment buildings, shopping centers, etc.) People who perceived the area in positive terms (calling it "beautiful," "natural," "pretty," etc.) were more likely to want to leave it in its present state as open space, make it into a park, or develop it with only single-family houses.

People who make decisions about how to use certain natural resources are the same way. Their perception of the natural environment tends to affect what they decide should be done with it.

Mrs. Hine is a cultural anthropologist doing research on participatory ecology with Dr. Luther Gerlach of the Department of Anthropology of the University of Minnesota.

Environmental perception is often quite an unconscious thing. And it has very little to do with scientific facts about the environment.

Community Standing

A second factor which affects decision-making is the position of the decision-maker in the social, political, and economic structure of the community. Here I am not talking about the obvious monetary benefits which the newspapers call "conflict of interest." I am talking about the difference between a decision-maker's personal feelings about the environment and the attitudes which he thinks should control his decisions as a business executive or government official.

An individual who has a keen appreciation of natural beauty and even some ecological awareness may find that he must make environmental decisions based instead on the well-known principle of minimax: minimize cost and maximize economic gain. Unless a decision-maker can give a monetary value to trees and water and green places, he feels that these cannot be "rationally" included in the decision.

Cultural Biases

A third factor which can cancel out or inhibit the use of scientific ecological information in decision-making are certain basic assumptions (biases if you will) which the decision-maker thinks "have made this country great." One is the orientation of our whole society toward what is vaguely known as progress. The most unpopular decision any government official or businessman can make is the decision to do nothing. Unfortunately, perhaps, the most appropriate course we should take, in certain areas, may require just that: suspension of action. Even if the purpose is an extended period of needed study, it means, in effect, a period of inaction. For some decision-makers this is intolerable. They are under powerful pressure to *act*. To stand still, in American thought, is to go backward.

Another basic idea, which incidentally is not shared by people in all countries, is that man is essentially an economic animal and that economic growth is by definition good. Closely related to this is the Western notion of unlimited goods. We are used to thinking that somehow with bigger and better machines there can be more of everything for everybody. But we are beginning to realize that bigger is not necessarily better and that growth for growth's sake is the principle of the cancer cell.

97

Cultural Adaptation.

A fourth factor that may make ecologically sound decisions difficult is the one thing that makes man different from all other species—his capacity to adapt to all sorts of environmental conditions. Most animals can live only in certain types of environments. But the human animal can adjust to all climates and all types of environments.

There is a real danger that man will respond to his present environmental crisis by simply adjusting gradually to worse and worse conditions. Residents of Los Angeles have become accustomed to smog even though their eyes water and their schoolchildren often can't have outdoor physical education classes. We can become accustomed to conditions that will kill us. Delay in decision-making is the way it can be done.

Consistent small delays during which our present methods of using natural resources are continued can lead to our gradual acceptance of gradually deteriorating environment. It is within the capacity of man to dream up values and explanations that make even dangerous levels of pollution seem inevitable or somehow right. If this occurs, man will have adapted to his own extinction.

People-Pressure

A final factor which may affect environmental decision-making in quite a different way is the full development of what some people call the "New Conservation" and others call "Ecology Action." Movements are something we have lots of today. They have very important effects on decision-makers.

A movement is characterized by what looks like total disorganization. Different groups within it have widely different ideas as to goals and use very different means to accomplish these goals. Participants in all movements engage in a great deal of infighting. In fact this very lack of centralized control and obvious factionalism give the deceptive appearance of no organization at all. These warring factions, however, are linked through overlapping memberships, personal ties between leaders, and the activities of "traveling evangelists." In the ecology movement Barry Commoner, Paul Ehrlich, and perhaps Gary Snyder are examples—though they would probably prefer to be called spokesmen than evangelists. Because of such linkages, factions within a movement have a disconcerting way of burying the hatchet and joining forces just when the opposition has written them off.

98

A movement is also characterized by total personal commitment on the part of a large number of participants. During the five years of research in different types of movements, we have found that in each there is what we have called a commitment process. "Conversion" is a word usually reserved for religion. But people become converted to movements through a very similar process. It includes some deeply moving experience which changes the individual's feelings about himself, his relationship with others, and sometimes his relationship with the natural environment also. Such an experience is usually accompanied by an action or series of actions involving some sort of risk. It might be quitting a job because of what you have come to believe. Or doing something you believe is right which other people ridicule you for. It may mean speaking out about something you believe is wrong even if this causes painful rifts between you and your friends or members of your family. It could be something that lands you in jail for what you believe. Commitment is something that you can't go back on—that sets you on a whole new course of life.

Such a committed individual is willing to take high risks and generates a remarkable ability to influence others to his way of thinking. Opponents of truly committed movement participants often view them as a social malady and their ideas as insidiously contagious.

At this stage of the game, the conservation-ecology movement has not generated enough of such commitment to make much of a dent on the decision-makers. If or when it does, it may become a very potent factor affecting environmental decision-making.

Conclusion

The people in our society who make important decisions about the environment in which we live can no longer afford to be blinded by their own personal feelings about a "swamp" or a "wasteland" when ecological facts require them to begin to look at that natural area differently. They can no longer put economic gain above environmental protection. And this goes for all of us, for we are all environmental decision-makers. We make decisions that affect the state of our environment every day of our lives. If we place monetary gain first over environmental health, we will find that economic gain will have destroyed the very thing we all get economic gain *from*: the natural life-support system in which we live—the world. None of us can any longer afford to just "get used to" bad conditions.

Decision-makers in our society are supposed to be responsive to the will of the people. If they are not, people must band together to make them so. This requires that citizens begin to look at their environment differently. We must let the new knowledge about ecology and about what we are doing to our life-giving environment change our own ways of thinking and our own personal habits. Then we must form groups of friends, neighbors, or the people we work with in order to put pressure on our decision-makers for better environmental protection. It is *our* environment and *our* lives that are at stake.

POLITICAL ECOTACTICS IN SOUTH FLORIDA

James Redford

The tactics you learn by trial and error are better remembered, but, hopefully, the valid experience of others will save a few steps.

Your education starts with a specific problem—a bay, a river, the air you breathe. The method of attack is your second decision; your first is whether the victory is worthy of the battle. Your *effective* appearances before commissions, boards, etc., are of finite number which can be overspent. Thus, if it is a rich piece of bay bottom you wish to preserve, possibly it is better to fight for the whole bay.

But nothing in human endeavor is absolute. Better that you make a decision even if it is the wrong one. So let's consider the bay bottom which some developer has decided to dredge and fill. Right or wrong, you choose a frontal attack on the issue.

One of the first axioms you should learn is that usually by the time of the public hearing, the issue has been decided. If you suspect that the decision is against you, it *can* be changed by massive public reaction at the meeting. But don't try the mass-reaction route too often. It gets less "massive" with use. It is better to lobby before the meeting, and, if possible, before the members of the board have made up their minds.

Remember, the lobbyist must know more than the "lobbied." Have your facts!

Now, let's say, you begin at the local level, with a hearing before the County Commission. You have spoken privately with all of your key commissioners prior to the meeting. You think you may have a chance of killing the proposed dredging, but you are not sure. Politicians and civil servants often have an elliptical way of response. It is still necessary to put on a good case even if you are sure of winning. Your

Mr. Redford is president of the Mangrove Chapter of the Izaak Walton League of America and is a former president of the Florida Division of the Izaak Walton League. He was the winner of the 1970 American Motors Conservation Award for 1970.

commissioners have to have a good public reason to vote for your side.

Line up your scientists. If you are using scientists of several specialties, try to put them in some logical order. Keep them as brief and unscientific as possible. Federal- and state-employed scientists are some of the best. While they are testifying, they are being paid, and their testimony has some weight in law. For example, state biologists and U.S. Fish and Wildlife Service biologists must make surveys before a dredge permit is granted. Today, the biological reports of the appropriate federal bureau can hold up development for a long time. Thus, the testimony of these scientists should carry a lot of weight at your hearing.

Introduce each of your scientists, then you yourself sum up at the conclusion of your case. If you have other pressure or voter groups to testify, let them come on after your summing-up. In this manner you will not be identified with any subsequent reckless statements or actions.

Assume that you "lose." Seldom do you ever completely lose. If you can keep your case going long enough, someone on some level of government will take up your cause.

Your next step is before the State Cabinet. If it is only a submerged land *sale* you are opposing, you are in good shape. Five votes are needed to authorize the sale. Only 55 acres were sold last year. But for a dredging permit, only a majority of those present is needed.

According to the Randell Act, a biological report is required before a permit to dredge and fill can be granted. This report is made by biologists of the State Department of Natural Resources. A hydrological report may be required, and this could be a device for a flank attack. The biological report is sent to the staff of the Internal Improvement Fund. The staff makes its recommendations after the biological report is completed, but the Trustees (the State Cabinet) are not bound by staff recommendations.

At this level, correspondence is most necessary. Cabinet members are somewhat impatient with submerged land problems and need the jog from "all those people out there" to remind them that there are others in this state besides lobbyists—or perhaps just different lobbyists. If you can personally lobby in Tallahassee, it is well to talk to that member of the Cabinet's staff who handles conservation matters. Of course, if you can get to the member himself, that is even better.

Suppose that the vote goes against you. You are still a long way from having a dead issue. You can now appeal to the federal level. The would-be-dredger must get a permit from the U.S. Army Corps of Engineers. They, in turn, must get a biological survey from the U.S. Fish and Wildlife Service at Vero Beach. By requesting them, you can get notices of all proposed dredgings in your area from the U.S. Army Corps of Engineers in Jacksonville. When yours is announced, get your correspondents active again. Demand a public hearing.

Let us assume that the engineers want to grant the permit, but you have persuaded the U.S. Fish and Wildlife Service to hold out against it. The procedure then is for the disagreement to progress upward through channels to the desks of the Secretary of the Interior and the Secretary of the Army. I don't know where it goes from there.

Now is the time you should be affiliated with some national conservation society. Your Washington conservation officer can work wonders for you. You should also be in touch with your elected officials in Washington, but, again, make sure that the victory is worth the war. Congressmen are selective and seldom make commitments in local controversies. Use them only for the heavy push.

Assume again that you lose. Then there are the courts, and, by this time, you should have a member of your organization who is a good attorney and is willing to help you without charge. By this time, of course, someone should have taken up your cause as a political issue. All of this will have taken much time, and surely an election will have been held during the controversy. Hopefully, your man will make it. Several of ours have.

Assume now that you win. You may still need your "good and free" lawyer. The would-be dredger could sue the Army Corps of Engineers and you should be ready to file as an intervenor. In this way, you can back up the Justice Department lawyers whose talents do not always match their intentions.

This has been a specific case, but there are several things which all cases have in common:

(1) They can be fought on several levels of government.

(2) They must be fought on all levels of government if you plan to seek remedy in court. This is what is known as "exhausting Administrative remedy."

We cannot consider every type of case—pollution, zoning, wildlife preserve, etc., so we will end with a few cautionary words.

Beware of megalomania!

It is probably necessary that one person in each area take the ecotactical leadership. Politicians like to identify an issue with a man. Whatever, the fact remains that some of the strongest conservation movements are run by one single person. Others can help if they will.

So, you have some significant successes in battling for ecology. I will tell you now that if you seek all the credit, your successes are over. Reputations in ecotactics are made from the accumulation of credit crumbs left over from many, many battles. Credit is the carrot you hold out when seeking what you want. In other words, you can't have what you want and keep the credit too. You should certainly hide your smile when, after years of repetition, you finally hear some civil servant or politician recite your words as his own. Take this as a measure of your success.

The direct or frontal attack is not always the most effective. A battle against a massive rezoning case is a recent example. What we desired was much less population density than proposed, preservation of a fringe of bay mangroves, etc. But population density has seldom been sufficient grounds for zoning application defeat, and the commission had previously turned down the mangrove fringe. The lack of sewage planning and the threat of withdrawal of federal grant-in-aid funds for treatment plants were what turned the tables—this plus massive citizen reaction.

Thus, temporarily, the desired end is achieved by a diversionary or flanking attack. It must be followed up, however, since nothing but the zoning application has been decided.

Another point of the eco-attack is the "Law of Parsimony." Conservation '70 did a fair job during the 1970 session of the Florida legislature in getting several good bills passed. But many great aims were missed, or nearly so, because of too many demands. For an example, the manta ray was protected, but excellent water pollution control bills died. Although many good things were accomplished, the session may not achieve what was accomplished by a single bill three years ago—namely, the Randell-Thomas Amendment to the Bulkhead Act. The lesson to be learned is a corollary of an earlier point—make the victory worth the battle.

It must sound ridiculous at this point to urge purity of motive, but this must be stressed. You can be as tricky as you like but never dirty. As I said before, the politician often identifies the issue with the man. The ends do not necessarily justify the means, but they often resemble them. And as a corollary to this, beware of the man who wants to win only on his own terms. The axe he is grinding is not yours.

Lastly, remember that the world is not made up of absolutes. You have your side, and your opponent has his. It is jejune to swear everlasting enmity because of one difference of opinion. If you play it right, the two of you could be together on the next issue while yielding nothing on this one. It has happened.

GROUPS WORKING TO SAVE SOUTH FLORIDA

Polly Redford

One individual alone cannot do much to preserve South Florida's environment. But the minute he joins with two or three others and calls himself an organization, his power increases a hundredfold. Many important battles have been won with a handful of people—for example, the blocking of a multimillion dollar oil refinery and industrial seaport on Biscayne Bay by twelve men and women with a post office box called Safe Progress Association.

In the long run, however, these *ad hoc* groups die off as new issues, new problems supercede old ones. Members who want to continue the environmental fight usually find themselves joining one or more of the "old line" conservation organizations. These are far from perfect, but they do offer many advantages that purely local groups cannot match: publications, literature, information services, research, professional assistance, representation in Washington.

At this writing in 1970, the three most active national organizations doing environmental work in South Florida are the Audubon Societies, the Izaak Walton League of America, the Nature Conservancy. To find the chapter nearest you, contact: National Audubon Society, 3370 Mary Street, Miami, Fla., 33133; Izaak Walton League, 2829 Bird Avenue, Miami, Fla. 33133; Nature Conservancy, 305 W. Beacon Road, Lakeland, Fla. 33803.

A new group, Zero Population Growth, Inc., 1035 San Pedro, Coral Gables, Fla. 33156, shows promise for the future, and so do several college student groups at area colleges and universities.

Learn about their local programs and platforms before joining,

South Florida author Polly Redford has been active for the past ten years in the Izaak Walton League and the Audubon Society. She and her husband James Redford were pioneers in the long fight to save Biscayne Bay by opposing the establishment of an oil refinery on the shores of south Biscayne Bay and were key figures in the establishment of Biscayne National Monument.

though, for local chapters vary widely from one county to another, and a name to be reckoned with in Palm Beach might, on the west coast, represent only a senior citizens' supper club. In some cases, you might prefer to join a national organization such as the Sierra Club, the Wilderness Society, or the Friends of the Earth which has no local chapter.

Conservation organizations are not the only ones to tackle environmental problems. The League of Women Voters, for example, has very strong programs on water quality and water pollution, so do some Kiwanis Clubs. Thus, lawyers and engineers might do more to improve Florida's air and water by forming strong pollution control committees in their local bar associations and engineering societies than by taking a nature study course. The same is true of women's clubs, garden clubs, student organizations, church groups, civic associations.

If you really want to help, assess yourself, your own talents. Where and how do you fit in best? That is the place to start. And whether or not you choose to join a regular conservation group, get to know them, plan to work with them, if only to avoid wasteful duplication of effort.

Since all environmental work is basically educational, what you're going to need most is *information.* You'll need facts and figures to convince your congressman or county commissioner that pesticides are poisoning the landscape before he'll pass laws against them. This is what Audubon, Izaak Walton, Nature Conservancy, Sierra Club, Sport Fishing Institute, Wilderness Society, etc., are set up to do. They'll be glad to help you get started.

INDIVIDUAL ACTION

Judith Voliner Wilson

What can I do to halt the pollution of air and water?

What can I do to help stop the drain on our nonrenewable resources?

What can I do to help ease the pressure on our living resources?

As the significance of our "environmental crisis" becomes increasingly clear, more and more people are asking these questions. The answers are not easy to live by in a society that places high value on personal convenience, in a society where individuals tend to assume that "they" are doing something about it all. Solutions to these problems will depend largely on each individual's willingness to accept his or her responsibility to change his own life style—to accept the challenge of living with a new code of values.

Population

The fact that human beings are multiplying far too rapidly to maintain any kind of reasonable balance within the system that supports us is, of course, the fundamental problem. Large families may be "natural," but we have, through our technological advances, overcome many of the "natural" factors that would limit our population growth. Living within a largely controlled environment demands that we control our numbers as well.

Changing Habits

Changing habits is never easy, especially when there is no immediate visible benefit from the change. The temptation to accept what is easiest is particularly strong when everyone around you seems to be doing just that with no apparent ill effects. But individual efforts, like

---

Mrs. Wilson worked with environmental planner Julia Allen Field for a number of years and is now in the Miami office of the National Audubon Society.

individual votes, *do* make a difference. Survival of the earth as we know it depends on finding the right answers to the problems facing us today, and each person, each family, is either a part of the problem or a part of the solution.

The Automobile

The automobile is a double threat—it consumes petroleum products (one of our rapidly disappearing nonrenewable resources) at an astonishing rate, and it is the single largest contributor to air pollution. When you buy a car look first for efficiency and long use. Keep your engine clean and in tune. Use lead-free gas if possible.

A system has been developed to convert standard engines at relatively low cost, to run on natural gas. This system cuts exhaust pollutants by over ninety percent, reduces engine wear, reduces operating costs, and is well worth investigating.

Of course, the surest way to limit fuel consumption and exhaust pollutants with your family car is to limit your use of the car. Share rides. Ride a bicycle. Walk. A car is a very expensive means of transportation—it is not a toy.

One of the most effective means of curtailing consumption and pollution by the automobile is an efficient mass transportation system. We have the technology to develop such a system now. Opposing new highways and parking facilities will help to make such a system a high priority issue. Inner-city driving is seldom a pleasure—as it becomes increasingly difficult to drive in the city, the need for a reasonable alternative will become more obvious. Development of a rapid mass transit system will be doubly effective if we insist upon use of some of the funds presently earmarked for highways. Here, the individual action that is going to count will be political action—but before going any further into the role each person must play in influencing community and legislative decisions, there are other areas where the individual can exercise his power as a consumer.

Consumer Action

When buying electric applicances careful consideration of economic use is imperative. Know how much electricity an appliance will use before you buy; there is often a great difference in the efficiency of similar products. Don't buy electric gadgets just for the fun of it. The companies that promote "all electric living" are the same companies that insist we must accept thermal pollution and potential radiation pollution because of increased consumer "needs."

New evaluations of potential pollutants in products on supermarket shelves appear frequently, and there is no need to include here long lists of detergent phosphate contents, alternatives to hard pesticides, or timetables on breakdown of various biodegradable products. As up-to-date lists and data on new products are published, read them, save them, and use them when you buy.

There are many excellent specific suggestions for concerned consumers in *The User's Guide to Environmental Protection,* published by Friends of the Earth/Ballantine Books and also in Betty Ann Ottinger's *What Every Woman Should Know—and Do—About Pollution: A Guide to Good Global Housekeeping,* published by EP Press, New York. Generally, rules to keep in mind while shopping include avoiding "throw-away" containers whenever possible, avoiding products with unnecessary plastic or cardboard wrappings (packages within packages, etc.), avoiding colored paper products (dyes pollute), avoiding gimmick containers (unnecessarily complex packaging—aerosols where simple refillable sprays will do the job—containers that insure waste as part of the product), looking for easily recycled packaging (aluminum rather than mixed-metal cans), and looking for returnable (reusable) bottles. Speak to your neighbors and the store manager about bulk purchasing (for instance, wine in barrels); if enough customers seem interested, stores will often buy in bulk for those who wish to bring their own containers.

Household Waste Control

While it is desirable to grow your own vegetables, save organic house and garden scraps for your own compost piles, and generally adopt a "back to nature" life style, for many this is impractical, if not impossible. Still, there are efforts everyone can and should make to maintain a household that places the least possible strain on the environment.

Even with careful, conscientious shopping an accumulation of cardboard and plastic containers and nonreturnable bottles and jars is inevitable. Reuse them. Think up new uses for them. If you can't use them, find someone who can; it may be an old mayonnaise jar to you, but to someone else it's a needed specimen jar. Making decorations and doll furniture from old salt boxes or stilts from coffee tins may not be your "thing," but to a teacher at a daycare center, or to a children's ward at a hospital, these "trash" items are tools to work with.

Many items that can't be reused can be recycled; newspaper and aluminum cans are two obvious examples. Depots for collecting trash for recycling exist in many neighborhoods now. These depots will increase in number and expand in the types of products they accept as awareness of the economic value of "trash" develops. These recycling depots are not only valuable aids in economic waste management and resource preservation—they are valuable educational aids. They can inform an entire community of a problem, of an economically feasible solution to the problem, and can encourage others to start following a more responsible course in their own household. Saving your newspapers and aluminum cans and turning them in for recycling will be an inconvenience until depots are more centrally located and in full-time operation, but the results are well worth the effort. The same basic rule that applies in encouraging a sound family budget, a stable economy, and in controlling inflation applies in running an ecologically sane household: in purchase, in use, and in disposal—*don't waste!*

Expanded Personal Responsibility

While efforts within individual households are important, the magnitude of the problems, and the degree to which industry and government agencies contribute to these problems (or lag in contributing to the solutions) extends the personal responsibility of every individual. There is an urgent need for voters to be well-informed, for them to know how to become effective participants in their government. Volunteers are needed for everything from scientific and legal research to talking to school groups, from typing to monitoring hearings. There is a need for every person to know where his or her talents can best be used.

Group Action

The best way to become and stay well informed is through one or more of the national or local conservation-oriented organizations. All of these groups need and deserve support. Find those whose range of interests seems most compatible with your own concerns and join them. If you haven't the time (or energy or inclination) to become really active within these groups, join anyway. Your financial support is essential to their being able to continue their work. Individual or family memberships are seldom expensive and should be a part of every person's budget.

Educational Action

Improving basic knowledge of our environment is important at all age levels. Through the various conservation groups, or through your PTA, you can find out what conservation courses are being taught in your local schools. Are they making full use of resources available through the country? Through the state? Through private organizations?

"Environmental education" is, or should be, a part of nearly every study area, from personal hygiene and basic science courses through geography and civics. Talk to teachers. Talk to principals. Push for a total program of knowledge of man's interaction with his environment —on the individual level, on the neighborhood or community level, on regional and national levels, on the whole-earth level. No matter what field a youngster will go into, this understanding is as essential as the traditional "three R's."

There is a need for both general and detailed studies in so many areas that teachers and students from high school age through graduate school can provide a real service through taking on environmental study projects. Gaps in our information exist in a surprising number of fields. Equally important are the gaps that exist between gathering the scientific data and making it available to the general public. Closing these gaps increases the total of available information and provides valuable experience for the students involved.

Political Action

Increased individual involvement in the legal and political aspects of environmental problem-solving and problem prevention is the most effective weapon we have. Knowledge of your government is the first essential. This begins with knowing your representatives at all levels of government. Find out what stands they've taken on specific environmental issues. Find out what their voting record has been. *All* candidates are "for conservation" and "against pollution"—but what have they actually *done* when faced with a conflict between environmental integrity and an immediate economic boost for their constituents? Many initially sound bills for protection of natural resources have been passed by "conservation-minded" legislators only after they have effectively rendered the bill useless by watering down in committee. Find out who the "good guys" and the "bad guys" are and *make your votes count.*

On many issues government representatives depend upon hearing from their constituents before making a firm decision on how to vote on an issue. They know that people who care enough to send a personal letter (as opposed to a form letter or a carbon copy) and sign their names are those who care enough to vote. Letters may be detailed evaluations of the pros and cons of an issue or they may simply urge support or defeat, but *every letter counts.* Don't make the mistake of writing only to those you feel are friendly to the cause—chances are their votes will be with you anyway, and many of those with "bad guy" reputations are looking for ways to improve their image. *The Voter's Guide to Environmental Politics,* another Friends of the Earth/Ballantine Book, is an excellent reference on citizens' political action. Many of the factors that influence decisions are out of the control of the average citizen, but everyone can and should write and let their wishes be known.

Action on Issues

When a community is faced with a specific environmental threat it is important to know how to go about fighting it. What pertinent laws are already on the books? Do they provide for strict enforcement? Is new or improved legislation really necessary? Or is the problem one of poor administration or enforcement? What officials will be most responsive to public pressure on the issue?

Know who has authority to make or enforce decisions. Know the chain of command within whatever government structures are involved. If you feel those on the local level will be (or have been) unresponsive, try to get a favorable stand at a higher level.

Find out where and when citizens can make their complaints or recommendations heard. Check with other concerned groups or individuals and try to coordinate your efforts. Be sure you have a solid argument based on scientific or economic fact when you present your case to those who will make the decision. If studies on the specific issue at hand do not exist, initiate them. Find friends qualified in whatever areas are involved and ask their help in preparing testimony.

Having solid facts to back your stand is most important. Emotional pleas for preservation of natural beauty have very little influence when the opposition starts a push for growth and development as an "economic boon to the community" or harps on the "prohibitive expense" of proper waste control.

When all the factors are considered, preservation of a unique area, careful land-use planning for remaining open spaces, and strict waste control laws are economically sound measures and make good sense in terms of long-range benefits to the community. Such arguments cannot be easily shrugged off by those making the decisions. Further, a sound argument set forth by reliable persons generally gets good press coverage. In a situation where citizen groups or concerned individuals often find themselves facing well-paid professional public relations men, this is very important.

Legal Action

Many problems can be solved through developing public awareness and using this pressure to encourage government action, but in an increasing number of instances, solutions can be found only through the courts. This type of action can range from formal objection to block potentially damaging land-use proposals (many of which must receive judicial approval) to filing suit against a major corporation or governmental agency for failure to comply with existing legislation.

In many instances groups can call on attorneys from their own membership to handle a case at cost, or to assist in preparation of a case. A few individual attorneys and law firms are willing to volunteer their services in cases involving environmental protection, but court action can still be extremely expensive. While few individuals can offer cash to help meet court costs, organizations often can.

Not everyone is qualified to research the legal aspects of a case involving environmental law, or to gather the necessary evidence to support such a case, but it's often surprising how much a concerned, informed citizen *can* contribute. It is an exciting type of action to become involved in for someone really willing to work.

Personal Commitment

Becoming involved in the movement for a better relationship between man and his environment is a personal commitment that cannot be made casually. Awareness of this relationship will make a difference in every aspect of your daily routine.

If you have the time and energy, it is possible to find yourself in a position of some influence in the decision-making process. Unfortunately, many effective workers are lost at this point. The temptation to avoid what may be a losing fight is particularly strong after a major success. But the work that needs to be done cannot be done without "rocking the boat." A firm stand on principles is occasionally a popular stand—where the leaders can become instant heroes. But such heroes must be willing to do battle for equally important but unpopular causes as well.

Whether the individual action you undertake is limited to your own household, or extends to a total career-level involvement, your true effectiveness will be limited only by your willingness to sacrifice personal convenience or public image for responsible action and integrity.

A FEW CONCLUDING REMARKS

Ross McCluney

In compiling a set of specialized articles by different authors, as is done in this book, it is not possible to obtain complete coverage of a multi-faceted subject and to maintain a continuity of style and logical progression throughout. This chapter is an attempt to fill in some of the missing links and to stress those which the editor feels are most important for the reader to understand and remember.

Most people by this time have heard enough about pollution and are anxious to see something substantial *done* about it. A discussion of citizen action is included at the end of this chapter. When approaching the solution of an environmental problem, it is extremely important for the individual involved to have the correct mental attitude about the problem. Let me give an example of what is meant by this.

The Engineering Mentality

During a recent flight low over the Everglades and the Big Cypress Swamp, I was extremely impressed by the enormous flatness of the land. During the summer and early fall rains, most of the region is covered with a thin sheet of water, extending for miles in all directions. From this observation alone, it becomes ridiculously obvious that digging a canal through the area, even if it is only a few feet deep, will have a profound effect on the natural water flow patterns of these interior flatlands.

The Army Corps of Engineers and other earlier engineers have done just that. They carved up South Florida with an extensive network of canals, pumps, dikes, and gates (see map p. 29), for the stated purpose of "flood control." As a result, much of the water that traditionally flowed south from the Lake Okeechobee area to the central wet prairies and on to the Everglades National Park is now diverted to the ocean and to coastal salt waters, away from the central portion of the peninsula.

As long as there is an abundance of rain the central regions do not suffer excessively. But with the coming of a severe dry season, such as the drought of early 1971, the lack of water becomes critical. The Everglades dries up sooner than normal, fires sweep the area more extensively than normal, and South Florida becomes a dry, parched desert with all the animals crowded together near the few sloughs and gator holes which are deep enough to still hold water.

No better example of what Gene Marine calls the "engineering mentality" can be found in South Florida. When faced with a serious environmental disaster created by their canal system, did the engineers admit their mistake and fill in the canals again? Did they try and return the land to its former natural state? No! They appealed to the absurd: They proposed the digging of *more* canals. They proposed to build *more* dikes, to raise the water level of Lake Okeechobee still further, in order to store more water for use in the dry season. And now, when faced with a water shortage in the Glades, they are proceeding to investigate weather modification—rainmaking—as a way to get back the water which was diverted to the sea by their canals in the first place.

The engineers propose one artificial solution on top of another. When faced with what they think is a problem, they immediately jump in to start constructing another "solution." To quote from *America the Raped* by Gene Marine:

> There is an engineers' way of looking at problems, an engineering approach to public questions, to planning, even to correcting the malfunctions that were introduced by the Engineers in the first place. It is the simple, supposedly pragmatic approach of taking the problem as given, ignoring or ruthlessly excluding questions of side effects, working out "solutions" that meet only the simplest definitions of the problem. It is an approach that never seeks out a larger context, that resents the raising of issues it regards as extraneous to the engineering problem involved.

This is the engineering mentality.

To paraphrase some remarks Gene Marine made in the article "The Engineering Mentality" which appeared in a recent issue of *Playboy Magazine*: The whole point of the water problem in South Florida can be grasped from a look at two maps of the state—a relief map and a population map. Almost all of the water is in Lake Okeechobee, the central wetlands, and the underground aquifer; the overwhelming majority of the people live on the coastal ridges. Problem: Get the water to the people. If you accept the problem, you have already been conned by the engineering mentality. In the first place, the problem could as easily have been stated: "Get the people to the water." or even: "If you don't have the people, you don't need the water." In the second place, it probably shouldn't have been stated as a problem at all. State it as a problem and your thinking starts in on solutions. Who says it is a problem to begin with? The engineers.

I give this example here, not because I think we can turn the clock back and instantaneously make most of the people disappear from South Florida. I do it to emphasize how thoroughly the engineering mentality has penetrated our past thinking. I do it with the hope that perhaps we can begin to extricate ourselves from the straightjacket this mentality imposes on our approach to environmental "problem-solving."

I do not wish to leave the reader with the mistaken impression that the engineering mentality applies only to engineers or that all engineers have it. Many non-engineers, for example city planners and government administrators, fall victim to the engineering mentality. A few good engineers understand the need for a broader view of the problems, who seek to determine *all* the consequences and side effects of their designs.

We cannot do away with engineering. We need it. It will help us to get out of the fix we are in. But we need a new approach to problem-solving, one which begins by questioning the very statement of the problem, one which is willing to look for other solutions to the problems, solutions which clearly lie outside the traditional realm of engineering. In particular, we need for the ecologists, the engineers, and the conservationists to get together, to exchange views, and to attempt to develop a new approach to environmental problem-solving.

There is another very important point made by Gene Marine. It is that we must not allow ourselves to be trapped by the fallacy of growth-rate planning. Too many of our leaders appeal to the so-called "statistical inevitability" of population growth to justify their expansionist desires. They say that *since* the population of South Florida will be thus and so by 1980, we must begin now to provide the housing, roads, water supply, and other essentials needed by them. What they don't consider is that we can also plan *not* to provide these so-called essential services, so that the population distribution will adjust itself to the situation and people will begin going elsewhere than South Florida.

Don't raise the level of Lake Okeechobee, don't dig the canals to get the extra water to the population centers, don't build more roads and highways, and the population of South Florida will *not* grow by thus and so. People and industries, learning that the area faces a water shortage, will go elsewhere. Some land speculators, of course, will lose out; but there's enough water so that South Florida can sustain its present population for generations—and the future of South Florida as a viable place to live may be assured by refraining from this massive ecological rape.

Transportation Mess

In the beginning, the automobile, with an interconnecting network of streets and highways, was an ideal solution to the transportation needs of the people. It provided reasonably rapid transportation (for short distances) together with a maximum of flexibility and freedom. One could go wherever he wanted, whenever he wanted, and by whatever route he wished to take. The automobile satisfied these goals quite well.

As the number of people and vehicles increased, however, the automobile began to lose more and more of its desirability as the most appropriate solution to our transportation needs. It should be quite obvious that as the multitudinous interconnecting roadways which cover a city begin to fill with traffic, freedom of movement, flexibility, comfort, safety, and accessibility begin to be severely restricted.

At some critical point, the automobile becomes not the *best* solution to the transportation needs of the people, it becomes the *worst* solution. The system becomes hopelessly clogged with traffic and no one can get anywhere in a reasonable length of time.

Faced with this threat, the automobile industry and the government should have seen what was coming and planned an acceptable alternative. It could have; it has some of the best engineering talent available. But it chose a different course of action. It chose to try and insulate the driver and to turn his attention away from the difficulties. It added air conditioning, power steering, automatic transmission, stereo sound, power brakes, and a host of other gadgets designed to make the driver worship his automobile rather than face up to its increasing inadequacy as an acceptable means of transportation. In a large measure the industry has succeeded.

And now, large-scale air pollution must be added to the list of insults which the automobile industry has thrown at the public. What do the wizards of industry do to "solve" this problem? They install hopelessly inadequate "air pollution control devices" on their cars. It's the engineering mentality all over again. Rather than backing off and looking at the overall problem, they proceed blindly with one engineering "fix" on top of another, each designed to "cure" the problem that the previous one created.

In foisting this inefficient system of transportation off on the public the industry is aided and abetted by governmental transportation agencies at all levels. Departments of transportation are almost universally caught in the growth-rate planning syndrome mentioned earlier. As the population increases they rush to meet the "need" with more and better streets and highways, carving up the land almost as viciously as do the engineers with their canals. They do not seem to realize that more expressways *stimulate* more traffic and encourage it. Even in their rush to meet the "demand" they are frequently inadequate. How many expressways have filled to near capacity within a few short months of their completion?

To give a local example of the dependence on the "statistical inevitibility" of population growth, Metro Traffic and Transportation Director, Eugene Simm, when questioned by a *Miami News* reporter about the traffic problems that would be created by a proposed new housing project in the Cocoplum area of Coral Gables, was quoted as follows: "The big thing is that we are right in there working with the developers on street capacity, access and traffic problems. The way we have to look at it is that development is going to come so we simply must make the best of it."

Because of the lack of far-sightedness, or perhaps the unwillingness of industry and government to look realistically at their future plans, we are now stuck with a terribly inadequate "system" of transportation that is so massive as to make it nearly impossible for us to convert to a more efficient system without painful large-scale disruptions. But convert we must, for, apart from the environmental impact of new streets and highways, the system will soon come grinding to a halt as it is on the verge of doing right now in downtown Chicago.

Regional Planning

Many people feel that proper regional planning will insure that development of a region will be based on sound environmental principles. Is this a realistic point of view? That depends upon one's definition of "proper" regional planning. In *The Architect and the City*, edited by Marcus Wiffen and published by the MIT Press, Ian McHarg states: "Planning has become dominated by economic determinism in which basic human objectives—health, beauty, community—have been assumed to be unmeasurable and are therefore discounted. Convenience and growth are the goals; efficiency and money are the criteria of excellence." Regional planning often ends up as planned abuse of the land. A regional land use plan is just what it says: a plan to use the land, and as such it often becomes a tool of the developer.

Seen in this light a land use plan can become a dangerous weapon, capable of inflicting great environmental destruction. Why whould we plan to *use* the land? We should be planning to *save* it. Instead of a Dade County Land-Use Master Plan, we should have a South Florida Regional Land Preservation Plan. But given the extreme power of the developers in South Florida, such a thing is practically impossible.

So we proceed pragmatically, conceding the need for *some* development and contenting ourselves with feeble and disorganized attempts to control the way in which it is allowed to occur. Perhaps we would be better off after all if we could get a South Florida Regional Plan put together by an interdisciplinary panel of ecologists, hydrologists, sociologists, agronomists, city planners, architects, and others having a real feeling for the importance of ecological and other environmental considerations, a feeling for the needs of both nature and the people.

In order for this to produce the desired environmental improvement, it will have to satisfy at least the following four basic requirements:

(1) The appropriate professional people (as defined above) must be appointed to the panel.

(2) The panel must decide on a maximum population which they feel the region can support.

(3) The recommendations of the panel must be formalized in a law which is legally binding on all.

(4) The law must be adequately enforced.

Until we can satisfy all four of these requirements we are probably better off with no regional planning at all.

A New Business Ethic?

One wonders what makes our business leaders doggedly persist with their environmentally damaging projects in spite of overwhelming scientific evidence that much of what they are doing is wrong. Why do they continue to search for specious arguments with which to deny their environmental wrongdoing, or to excuse it once recognized?

The answer lies in their historic devotion to expanding corporate profits as the ultimate goal, a goal they place above all other values, including environmental protection. This is the system. This is the way things are done, and it continues to play havoc with the environment, with the public's needs, and with the taxpayer's money which must be used to finance the costly repairs.

If you can't replace the system, perhaps you can turn it around on itself and find a way to use it effectively for environmental improvement. There are those who feel that this is a hopeless impossibility. If they are right, then only a massive, large-scale, environmentally-induced disruption of the economy can turn things around and force business to undertake the needed environmental housekeeping. If they are wrong, the disruption may not be necessary.

It is time for a new business ethic. If we can find a way to convince our business leaders of the seriousness of the environmental crisis and to show them how continued environmental degradation will eventually cut into their corporate profits, then we will be able to appeal to their sense of responsibility. We must then show them how it will be cheaper in the long run for them to mend their environmentally destructive ways. If we do, we may begin to see a slight change in the business ethic and a perceptible trend toward genuine environmental reform in business.

Conservationists are Survivalists

In reading this book one is apt to wonder why the Everglades and the Big Cypress Swamp are so strongly emphasized. These are wilderness areas, mostly inhabited by birds, fishes, and other land animals. They are relatively free of human inhabitants. Does this emphasis imply that the animals inhabiting these areas are more important than the people inhabiting the coastal highlands? Asked this way the question is poorly phrased. It is not just the animals in the wilderness areas that are important, it is the whole ecological system that we are concerned about. The animals are only a part of the system and are indicators of its condition. Destruction of the ecological balance in the wilderness areas will be ultimately more disastrous than would be the disruption of the ecology of the coastal highlands. Both the wilderness areas and the inhabited areas are important. The coastal areas are important to us, for they are where we live. The wilderness areas are also important to us, because their continued ecological strength is what makes our comfortable life along the coast possible.

Conservationists living along the coast are not preservationists just for the sake of preservation. They are survivalists. They wish to preserve the interior regions in order to insure the survival of the coastal areas as comfortable living places for themselves and other people.

In his book *Living by the Land,* published by Grove House in 1945, South Florida author John Gifford put it as follows:

> Unlike other mammals, man tries to dominate all creatures and to accumulate wealth to expand his power. Men all over the world are very much alike, except for certain variations that indicate their adaptation to climate, to forested mountains, broad plains, cities, and seashores.
>
> The pleasure of possession is so strong that not only individuals and groups of people but even nations are constantly clashing. Private interests and public interests are constantly at war. The haves fight the have-nots to preserve their gains. There is the age-old fight between private greed and public welfare. It is the age-old fight between good and evil, between the golden rule and the rule of gold, between construction and destruction as personified in Jehovah and Satan. Conservation is part of this struggle; it fights for those things which will benefit the greatest number of present *and coming* generations. It is unselfish; its main aim is the preservation and maintenance of the general public welfare.

According to this we should all become conservationists, working to save what little wilderness we have left.

Conservation 70's

Conservation 70's, Inc., is a coalition of groups and individuals whose primary objective is saving Florida's endangered environment. C-70's is primarily concerned with proposing, and then lobbying for, packages of environmental legislation to the Florida Legislature. It was organized in 1969, with the objective of political activism for environmental protection over a ten-year period—the decade of the seventies. By 1980, the founders reasoned, they will have achieved their goal or failed, in which case it will be too late to do anything.

In its first year of operation C-70's proved that it can be effective. Although the environmental lobby's package of fifty-five bills was too bulky, an almost unbelievable forty-one made it through the 1970 legislature. Although some were heavily amended, none were changed to a degree that the original intent was lost. Although few of the bills were properly financed, the fact that forty-one measures proposed by a single lobby could make it through a single legislative session is possibly unmatched anywhere. Most of the bills which passed will have a significant effect on environmental improvement in South Florida.

Among the laws that passed are:

Oil spill penalty and prevention.
Strict control of sewage outfall systems.
Protection of state-owned submerged lands.
Private riparian upland owners must consent before dredging, draining, or filling for public purposes.
No dredging in any navigable waters without a permit.
Increase in maximum penalty for pollution violation.
Police powers to Game and Fresh Water Fish Commission agents.
Constitutional amendment permitting state bonds to finance sewage control facilities.
Partial DDT ban.
Creation of an Environmental Education Coordinator.
Creation of a State Wilderness System.
Banning sale of alligator products.

In its second year of operation C-70's will be proposing new environmental legislation and pushing for state funding of the programs which passed in the last session. In this effort C-70's will need the support of the public, in the form of financial contributions and support of its proposed legislation. To find out just what C-70's is doing, write to:

Conservation 70's
Suite 326, Dorian Building
319 South Monroe Street
Tallahassee, Florida, 32304

Then spread the word. Contact South Florida legislators and begin working with them so that they will be properly informed about the activities of C-70's.

124

Getting to Know the South Florida Landscape

Reading this book and looking at its maps should be a good introduction to South Florida's environmental problems. But this is certainly not enough to develop a thorough understanding of these problems. There can be no adequate substitute for personal, close-up inspection of the problem areas.

Take the family or some friends with you and go exploring. Visit some of the places mentioned in this book. Take a leisurely trip along Alligator Alley or the Tamiami Trail, making frequent stops and inspecting Flood Control District canals, levees, and gates. Take an airboat ride. Visit Everglades National Park and take a guided tour. Drive to the Keys, rent a boat or trailer or take your own, and explore the estuaries and mangrove hammocks in the southern portion of the Park. Take a boat trip the length of Biscayne Bay and note the changes in water quality along the way. You might even visit some of the better-known polluters in South Florida. Ask for guided tours and don't be afraid to ask embarrassing questions.

If you would like some expert guidance on your field trips, make use of the many guided nature tours which are available in South Florida. In addition to its regular guided tours, the Everglades National Park is offering two unique backcountry tours. One, called Boat-a-Cades, involves South Florida boat owners in conducted boat trips into remote and interesting areas of the Park. The Saturday Boat-a-Cades begin at Flamingo and Everglades City and are led by Ranger patrol boats, giving participants an opportunity to learn many things about estuarine areas and their vegetation and wildlife. The similar Canoe-a-Cades follow routes through wilderness water trails and are varied throughout the year. Rental canoes are available at the starting point in Flamingo. For more information phone or write the Everglades National Park and request information about its guided tours. The address is: P.O. Box 279, Homestead, Florida 33030.

The Metropolitan Dade County Park and Recreation Department has several interesting nature tours which are open to the public. They are conducted, without charge, by naturalists of the Outdoor Education Staff from October through May. Both a nature walk and a bird walk are available at Greynolds Park in North Dade. Redland Tours begin at the Redland Fruit and Spice Park in South Dade. A weekly nature walk is scheduled at Camp Owaissa Bauer just north of Homestead. This hammock is particularly rich in lush native ferns and has an abundance of interesting solution holes, a geologic feature of the South Florida terrain. Adjacent to the hammock is a typical pineland habitat.

A Crandon Beach walk is conducted at the Bear Cut area and covers a brief introduction to the world of marine biology. The ecology of the area is stressed. A Matheson Hammock tour covers the hammock trails located on the west side of Old Cutler Road. Native plant and animal life of the South Florida hammocks will be pointed out. For further information on these programs, write or phone the Outdoor Education Program of the Dade County Park and Recreation Department at 50 S.W. 32 Road, Miami, Florida 33129. Fairchild Tropical Garden, located adjacent to Matheson Hammock Park in South Dade, offers the opportunity to observe a large number of native and imported species of tree and plant life.

Several South Florida conservation organizations offer a number of well-organized guided nature trips to their members and to the public. The Tropical Audubon Society has a very popular series of such trips which are always well-attended by its members. Look for other agencies and organizations offering guided tours to individuals and groups. The Pinejog Conservation Education Center in West Palm Beach has a number of valuable programs which involve both classroom and field study of environmental topics. Suggest that your child's school teacher take the class on a nature study field trip and volunteer to help her with the project.

Whenever you take a guided field trip do not hesitate to ask questions about the things you see which interest you. Ask how pollution and other environmental threats affect the particular area you are visiting. What is the most dangerous threat to the area and how long does the tour guide think the region can survive the danger?

Finally, explore your own neighborhood. Find out where your garbage and sewage go. Does your household use a septic tank? If so is there a canal or freshwater well nearby? If not, what kind of treatment, if any, does your sewage receive before it is released to the environment? Where is the outfall located?

What are the sources of air pollution that affect you? Is traffic congestion and population density increasing in your neighborhood? Are there community parks and recreation facilities? Are any being developed and planned? What land rezoning and development are occurring? Will the rezoning tend to degrade the environment? Who owns the land and who will be making the profits from its development? What overall benefits do people enjoy and desire from living in your community? What will your community look like in five or ten years at the present rate of growth and planned expansion? What burdens will this place on community facilities, your quality of living, and your taxes?

What Can I Do?

A question you might ask (and one often heard after an inspiring and moving lecture on environmental problems) is "What can *I* do? " Support of Conservation 70's and other environmentally active organizations has already been suggested here and in the article by Polly Redford. But you should begin by finding out all you can about the issues and problems facing us, including field trips to the problem areas whenever possible, as already suggested in this article. A bibliography is included at the end of this article to help you in becoming informed about the issues.

You should then determine what kind of involvement most suits your own talents and interests. You may be good at research and preparation of testimony for public hearings. Or you may be good at organizing an anti-pollution products fair or ecology carnival. The article by Judy Wilson should help you in selecting the kind of action that is best for you. Whatever you choose, the most important thing for you to do is to *get* involved and *stay* involved.

Most of our environmental problems cover large areas and involve large numbers of people. Overcoming them can probably only be accomplished by massive, large-scale programs of environmental reform. Ultimately, in this author's view, only the federal government will have the capability and power to exercise the leadership necessary to carry out these programs. Whether it *will* take the leadership depends upon our ability to stimulate enough public pressure to get the needed programs going and see that they are kept moving as long as the need exists. We shall all have to work hard to provide the grassroots support needed to sustain this effort.

SELECTED BIBLIOGRAPHY

General

(1) *America the Raped,* by Gene Marine. Avon Books Division of the Hearst Corporation, New York, 1969, $1.25. The whole sad story of how human folly has despoiled the American environment, primarily for private profit. Subtitled: "The Engineering Mentality and the Devastation of a Continent."

(2) *Moment in the Sun,* by Robert Rienow and Leona Train Rienow. Ballantine Books, New York, 1967, $.95. A report on the deteriorating quality of the American environment.

(3) *Science and Survival,* by Barry Commoner. The Viking Press, New York, 1966, $1.65. Dangerous flaws in the structure of science threaten our existence.

(4) *The Environmental Handbook,* ed. by Garrett De Bell. Ballantine Books, 1970. A compilation of essays prepared for the first national environmental teach-in.

(5) *The Frail Ocean,* by Wesley Marx. Ballantine Books, New York, 1967, $.95.

(6) *So Human an Animal,* by René Dubos. Charles Scribner's Sons, New York, 1970, $2.25.

(7) *A Sand County Almanac, With Essays on Conservation from Round River,* by Aldo Leopold. Ballantine Books, New York, 1966, $.95.

(8) *What Every Woman Should Know—and Do—About Pollution. A Guide to Good Global Housekeeping,* by Betty Ann Ottinger. EP Press, 116 Sullivan St., New York, 1970, $1.95. A delightful little book that everyone should read. It is printed on recycled paper.

South Florida

(1) *Environmental Problems in South Florida.* A report of the Environmental Study Group of the National Academies of

Science and Engineering, Washington, D.C. Dated March 1970, this booklet is an excellent semi-technical discussion of the major environmental problems of South Florida, particularly as they relate to the Everglades jetport.

(2) *The Trees of South Florida, Volume I: The Natural Environments and Their Succession,* by Frank C. Craighead, Sr. In preparation, University of Miami Press, Coral Gables, Florida.

(3) *The Everglades: River of Grass,* by Marjory Stoneman Douglas. Rinehart, New York, 1947; reprint Hurricane House Publishers, Inc., Coconut Grove.

(4) *On Preserving Tropical Florida,* by John C. Gifford; ed. and with an introduction by Elizabeth Rothra. In preparation, University of Miami Press, Coral Gables.

(5) *Environmental Impact of the Big Cypress Swamp Jetport,* United States Department of the Interior, September 1969. This is the "Leopold Report" and is available from either of the following two offices: U.S. Geological Survey, 903 West Tennessee St., Tallahassee, Florida 32304 and U.S. Geological Survey, Room 730, Federal Building, 51 S.W. 1 Ave., Miami, Florida 33130.

(6) *Some Hydrologic and Biologic Aspects of the Big Cypress Swamp Drainage Area, Southern Florida 1970,* United States Department of the Interior, U.S. Geological Survey, Water Resources Division. Available from the U.S.G.S. Miami office (address given above).

(7) *A Synoptic Survey of Limnological Characteristics of the Big Cypress Swamp, Florida,* United States Department of the Interior, Federal Water Quality Administration, Southeast Region, Southeast Water Laboratory, Technical Services Program, May 1970. Available from Federal Water Quality Administration, Technical Services Program, Southeast Water Laboratory, Athens, Georgia 30601.

(8) "The Role of Tidal Marshes in Estuarine Production," by E. P. Odum. Contribution No. 29 from University of Georgia Marine Institute. Reprinted, *New York State Conservationist,* June-July, 1961.

(9) "Water Off and On," by William E. Green, F. C. MacNamara, and Francis M. Uhler. In *Waterfowl Tomorrow,* U.S. Department of the Interior, 1964.

(10) "Notes on Biscayne Bay, Florida," by Hugh M. Smith. Appendix 2

130

of Report of the Commissioners of Fish and Fisheries, 1896, Washington, D.C.

(11) "The Role of the Alligator in Shaping Plant Communities and Maintaining Wildlife in the Southern Everglades," by F. C. Craighead. In *Florida Naturalist*, Nos. 1 and 2, 1968.

(12) *That Vanishing Eden, A Naturalist's Florida*, by Thomas Barbour. Little Brown and Co., Boston, 1944.

(13) *Florida Wild Life*, by Charles Torrey Simpson. MacMillan Co., New York, 1932.

(14) *From Eden to Sahara: Florida's Tragedy*, by John Kunkel Small. New York, privately printed, 1929.

(15) *A Guide to the Wilderness Waterway of the Everglades National Park*, by William Truesdell. University of Miami Press, in cooperation with the Everglades Natural History Association, Coral Gables, Florida, 1969, spiralbound, $2.50.

(16) *Boater's Guide to the Upper Florida Keys: Jewfish Creek to Long Key*, by John O'Reilly. University of Miami Press, in cooperation with the Everglades Natural History Association, Coral Gables, Florida, 1970, spiralbound, $2.50.

(17) *Orchids and Other Air Plants of the Everglades National Park*, by F. C. Craighead, Sr. University of Miami Press, in cooperation with the Everglades Natural History Association, Coral Gables, Florida, 1964, paper, $2.00.

(18) *Everglades—The Park Story*, by William B. Robertson, Jr., University of Miami Press, in cooperation with the Everglades Natural History Association, paper, $1.00.

(19) *Man in the Everglades: 2,000 Years of Human History in the Everglades National Park*. University of Miami Press, in cooperation with the Everglades Natural History Association, Coral Gables, Florida, 1968, cloth, $4.95; paper, $2.95.

(20) *A Naturalist in Southern Florida*, by Charlotte Orr Gantz. In preparation, University of Miami Press, Coral Gables, Florida.

The Population Explosion

(1) *The Population Bomb*, by Paul Ehrlich. Ballantine Books, New York, 1968, $.95. THE book on the global effects of overpopulation.

(2) *Population, Resources, Environment: Issues in Human Ecology*, by Paul R. and Anne H. Ehrlich. W. H. Freeman and Company, San

Francisco, 1970. Gives background and extends the concepts of *The Population Bomb.*

(3) *Population, Evolution, and Birth Control,* by Garrett Hardin. W. H. Freeman & Co., San Francisco, 1969, $2.95.

(4) *Famine—1975,* by William and Paul Paddock. Little, Brown and Co., 1967, $2.35. The Paddock brothers conclude that, because of overpopulation and depletion of natural resources, the world will be faced with the first of a series of global famines.

Air and Water Pollution

(1) *Air Pollution Primer,* published by the National Tuberculosis and Respiratory Disease Association, New York, 1969. Free from any local NTRDA office. An excellent introduction to the fundamentals of air pollution.

(2) *The Vanishing Air,* by John C. Esposito. Grossman Publishers, New York, 1970, $.95. The Ralph Nader Study Group report on air pollution.

(3) *Poisons in the Air,* by Edward Edelson and Fred Warshofsky. Pocket Books, New York, 1966, $1.00.

(4) *Air and Water Pollution,* ed. by Gerald Leinwald. Washington Square Press, New York, 1969, $.75.

(5) *Our Environment* Can *be Saved,* by Nelson A. Rockefeller. Doubleday and Company, New York, 1970, $5.95.

Transportation

(1) *Strategy for Mobility* ($5.00) and *Metropolitan Transportation Problem* ($6.00), both by Wilfred Owen. Brookings Institution, 1775 Massachusetts Ave., N.W., Washington, D.C., 1966.

(2) *Urban Transportation Problem,* by John R. Meyer. Harvard University Press, 1965, $11.95.

(3) *S/S/T and Sonic Boom Handbook,* by William A. Schurchliff. Ballantine Books, New York, 1970, $.95.

Resources and Solid Waste Management

(1) *Resources and Man,* by the Committee on Resources of the National Academy of Sciences. W. H. Freeman & Co., San Francisco, 1969.

(2) *Famine—1975,* by William and Paul Paddock. Little, Brown, and Co., Boston, 1967, $2.35. Because of overpopulation and

depletion of natural resources, the world will be faced with the first of a series of global famines in the year 1975.

(3) *Population, Resources, Environment: Issues in Human Ecology,* by Paul R. and Anne H. Ehrlich. W. H. Freeman & Co., San Francisco, 1970.

(4) *The Waste Makers,* by Vance Packard. Pocket Books Division of Simon and Schuster, New York, 1960, $.75.

Land Use

(1) *Design with Nature,* by Ian McHarg. Natural History Press, Garden City, N.Y., 1969, $19.95. The foremost statement of ecologically sound principles of land use planning.

(2) "The Ecology of the City," by Ian McHarg. From *The Architect and the City,* ed. by Marcus Wiffen. M.I.T. Press, Cambridge, 1966.

(3) *The Last Landscape,* by William H. Whyte. Doubleday and Company, Garden City, 1968. Chapter 11, "The Design of Nature," is especially good.

(4) *On Preserving Tropical Florida,* by John C. Gifford, ed. and with an introduction by Elizabeth Rothra. In preparation, University of Miami Press, Coral Gables, Florida.

(5) *God's Own Junkyard,* by Peter Blake. Holt, Rinehart, and Winston, New York, 1964. Subtitled: "The Planned Deterioration of America's Landscape."

Individual and Group Action

(1) *What Every Woman Should Know—and Do—About Pollution. A Guide to Good Global Housekeeping,* by Betty Ann Ottinger. EP Press, 116 Sullivan St., New York, 1970, $1.95.

(2) *The User's Guide to the Protection of the Environment,* by Paul Swatek. Ballantine Books, New York, 1970, $1.25.

(3) *The Voter's Guide to Environmental Politics,* ed. by Garret De Bell. Ballantine Books, New York, 1970, $1.95.

(4) *Environmental Action Projects for Clubs and Organizations.* Available free of charge from the Center for Urban Studies, University of Miami, Coral Gables, Florida 33124.

(5) *Ecotactics: The Sierra Club Handbook for Environment Activists,* ed. by John G. Mitchell with Constance Stellings. Pocket Books Division of Simon and Schuster, New York, 1970, $.95.

(6) *The Environmental Handbook,* ed. by Garret De Bell. Ballantine Books, New York, 1970, $.95.

(7) *Community Action for Environmental Quality,* by the Citizens Advisory Committee on Environmental Quality. Available from U.S. Government Printing Office, Washington, D.C. 20402, $.60.